MINOR WHITE

MINOR WHITE

A Living Remembrance

ANSEL ADAMS, ROBERT ADAMS, CHARLES ARNOLD,
ROBERT BOURDEAU, ISABEL KANE BRADLEY,
HARRY CALLAHAN, PAUL CAPONIGRO, WALTER CHAPPELL,
CARL CHIARENZA, JUDY DATER, ABE FRAJNDLICH, ARTHUR FREED,
ARNOLD GASSAN, WILLIAM GILES, ROBERT HAIKO,
NICHOLAS HLOBECZY, DAVID HORTON, WILLIAM LARUE,
PETER LAYTIN, ROGER LIPSEY, ROBERT MAHON, BARBARA MORGAN,
HAVEN O'MORE, SHIRLEY PAUKULIS, EDWARD RANNEY,
EUGENE RICHARDS, DR. ARNOLD RUSTIN, AARON SISKIND,
FREDERICK SOMMER, DRID WILLIAMS, JOHN YANG

AN APERTURE BOOK

Library of Congress Catalog Card Number: 58-30845. ISBN: 0-89381-161-0.

Aperture publishes a periodical, books, and portfolios to communicate with serious photographers and creative people everywhere. A complete catalogue will be mailed upon request. Address: Millerton, New York 12546.

This publication was supported by a grant from the National Endowment for the Arts, Washington, D.C., a federal agency.

The Minor White Archives, at Princeton University, includes all of the artist's photographic work, as well as his library and papers and his collection of photographs by other artists. Inquiries regarding this material should be addressed to The Minor White Archives, The Art Museum, Princeton University, Princeton, New Jersey 08544.

Photograph opposite page:
Abe Frajndlich, [Minor White] *Close-Up Eyes, 203 Park Avenue, March 21, 1976*

His camera-art is an eye, not in the banal sense that has plagued photography as a mechanical rival of painting, but in the sense of the eye as the most personal and responsive organ of the human face. I think of Schiller's riddle about the eye: "Kennst du das Bild auf zartem Grunde?"

It illuminates without burning.
It absorbs the whole cosmos.
The sky itself is depicted
Within its marvelous compass.
And yet what shines from it
Is more beautiful than what it receives.

It is the eye in which the world
  is impressed.
It is your eye if it looks at me with love.

MEYER SCHAPIRO,
from a commentary on Minor White

THE COMMUNITY OF INTEREST, the circle of intense, creative commitment that Minor White helped sustain and that sustained him during his lifetime, is suggested in this book dedicated to the multiple spheres of his influence. Many colleagues, students, and friends have contributed their photographs and have offered remembrances of Minor. Regrettably, not all of the contributions could be included, but each has in its own way been a sustaining force in our effort to pull together the delicate threads of Minor's complex life and to create a pattern that suggests certain qualities meaningful to the man and embodied in his lifelong devotion to photography. We have drawn deliberately on Minor's techniques, allowing unexpected correspondences and seemingly chance encounters to enter the process of envisioning, gathering, and editing this tribute. In the end we allowed for a sense of Minor's strength, his gentleness and loving kindness, his conflicts and frustrations, and his rich relationships to be suggested in this issue as a living remembrance—a way of continuing the qualities of his life and spirit worth cherishing.

THE EDITORS

Judy Dater, *Minor White, Undated*

What may be the deepest meanings of the images shown are not always easily recognizable at first glance. They emerge with increasing clarity only as we experience them. They take on a living reality to the degree that we are able to penetrate the mask that hides us from ourselves.

DOROTHY NORMAN, from *The Heroic Encounter*

Imogen Cunningham, *Minor White, Undated*

The creative process, so far as we are able to follow it at all, consists in the unconscious activation of an archetypal image, and in elaborating and shaping this image into finished work. By giving it shape, the artist translates it into the language of the present, and so makes it possible for us to find our way back to the deepest springs of life. Therein lies the social significance of art; it is constantly at work educating the spirit of the age, conjuring up the forms in which the age is most lacking. The unsatisfied yearning of the artist reaches back to the primordial images in the unconscious which are best fitted to compensate the inadequacy and one-sidedness of the present. The artist seizes on this image, and in raising it from the deepest unconsciousness he brings it into relation with conscious values, thereby transforming it until it can be accepted by the minds of his contemporaries according to their powers. . . . The artist's relative lack of adaptation turns out to his advantage; it enables him to follow his own yearnings far from the beaten path, and to discover what it is that would meet the unconscious needs of his age.

CARL JUNG, from "On the Relation of Analytical Psychology to Poetry"

Sitting on the radiator in the little back room of An American Place six months after World War II, we talked about how to make photographs, spoke about the Equivalent. Stieglitz said something or other about photography that makes visible the invisible, and something else about true things being able to talk to each other. His talk itself was a kind of equivalent; that is, his words were not related to the sense he was making. If anyone had ever talked like that to me before, I certainly had not heard him. In a few minutes he broke open the lump of poured concrete that had sunk me to the bottom of the Leyte Gulf. "Have you ever been in Love? . . . Then you can photograph."

MINOR WHITE, "Memorable Fancies," New York City, February 1946

An abstract picture is one which is completely free of extraneous associational appeal—hence, one in which the reality of art is present in its greatest purity. If an abstract picture is less powerful than a realistic one, it is because its art is less powerful; the power of the realist is not a result of his realism. I am enabled to say this because of Stieglitz's photographs, many of which are abstractions in the sense they do not present images of physical objects. To say that a photograph does not present an image means that the image of the thing has only the significance that paint has as paint. Such abstraction existing so clearly particularly in photography is a challenging commentary on all art. It is Stieglitz speaking.

EVELYN HOWARD, "The Significance of Stieglitz for the Philosophy of Science,"
from *America and Alfred Stieglitz*, 1934

Alfred Stieglitz, *Equivalent, 1930*

Man (looking at a Stieglitz Equivalent): Is this a photograph of water?
Stieglitz: What difference does it make of what it is a photograph?
Man: But is it a photograph of water?
Stieglitz: I tell you it does not matter.
Man: Well, then is it a picture of the sky?
Stieglitz: It happens to be a picture of the sky. But I cannot under-stand why that is of any consequence.

Conversation recorded by Dorothy Norman

Minor White, *Burning Tires, San Francisco, 1953*

The major sources of equivalent and metaphoric images in photography are the great forms of erosion that shape and reshape the world. Camera has a positive genius for turning the effects of weathering into beauty and equivalence: wood, stone, faces, ice. It grandly celebrates the forces themselves: light, snow, wind, space, water, fire, earthquake, bulldozer, dynamite.

MINOR WHITE, *Octave of Prayer*, 1972

Minor White, *Ladder and Door, Lincoln, Vermont, 1968*

From "Equivalence: The Perennial Trend"

MINOR WHITE

PROBABLY THE MOST MATURE IDEA ever presented to picture-making photography was the concept of Equivalence which Alfred Stieglitz named early in the 1920s and practiced the rest of his life. The idea has been continued by a few others, notably at the Institute of Design in Chicago under Aaron Siskind and Harry Callahan, and at the former California School of Fine Arts in San Francisco under the efforts of the present author. As a consequence, the theory is in practice now by an ever increasing number of devoted and serious photographers,

Walter Chappell, *Dutch Elm Tree Massacre, Rochester, 1957*

both amateurs and professionals. The concept and discipline of Equivalence *in practice* is simply the backbone and core of photography as a medium of expression-creation.

At one level, the graphic level, the word "Equivalence" pertains to the photograph itself, the visible foundations of any potential visual experience with the photograph itself. Oddly enough, this does not mean that a photograph which functions as an Equivalent has a certain appearance, or style, or trend, or fashion. Equivalence is a function, an experience, not a thing. Any photograph, regardless of source, might function as an Equivalent to someone, sometime, someplace. If the individual viewer realizes that for him what he sees in a picture corresponds to something within himself—that is, the photograph mirrors something in himself—then his experience is some degree of Equivalence. (At least such is a small part of our present definition.)

While we are reluctant to disappoint the reader by not giving some rules or signposts by which one can spot an Equivalent twenty feet away, we would rather be true to the facts of the situation than distort them. So at this graphic level of Equivalence no specifications will be listed.

At the next level the word "Equivalence" relates to what goes on in the viewer's mind as he looks at a photograph that arouses in him a special sense of correspondence to something that he knows about himself. At a third level the word "Equivalence" refers to the inner experience a person has while he is remembering his mental image after the photograph in question is not in sight. The remembered image also pertains to Equivalence only when a certain feeling of correspondence is present. We remember images that we want to remember. The reason why we want to remember an image varies: because we simply "love it," or dislike it so intensely that it becomes compulsive, or because it has made us realize something about ourselves, or has brought about some slight change in us. Perhaps the reader can recall some image, after the seeing of which he has never been quite the same.

Let us return for a moment to the graphic level of the photographic equivalent. While we cannot describe its appearance, we can define its function. When any photograph functions for a given person as an Equivalent we can say that at that moment and for that person the photograph acts as a symbol or plays the role of a metaphor for something that is beyond the subject photographed. We can say this in another way: when a photograph functions as an Equivalent, the photograph is at once a record of something in front of the camera and simultaneously a spontaneous symbol. (A "spontaneous symbol" is one which develops automatically to fill the need of the moment. A photograph of the bark of a tree, for example, may suddenly touch off a corresponding feeling of roughness of character within an individual.)

When a photographer presents us with what to him is an Equivalent, he is telling us in effect, "I had a feeling about something and here is my metaphor of that feeling." The significant difference here is that what he had a feeling about was not for the subject he photographed, but for something else. He may show us a picture of a cloud, the forms of which expressively correspond to his feelings about a certain person. As he saw the clouds he was somehow reminded of the person, and probably he hopes that we will catch, in the expressive quality of the cloud forms, the same feeling that he experienced. If we do and our feelings are similar to his, he has aroused in us what was to him a known feeling. This is not exactly an easy distinction to make, so maybe we can repeat. When the photographer shows us what he considers to be an Equivalent, he is showing us an expression of a feeling, but this feeling is not the feeling he had for the object that he photographed. What really happened is that he *recognized* an object or series of forms that, when photographed, would yield an image with specific suggestive powers that can direct the viewer into a specific and known feeling, state, or place within himself. With constantly metamorphizing material such as water or clouds or ice, or light on cellophane and similar materials, the infinity of forms and shapes, reflections and colors, suggests all sorts and manners of emotions and tactile encounters and intellectual speculations that are supported by and formed by the material but which maintain an independent identity from which the photographer can choose what he wishes to express.

The power of the equivalent, so far as the expressive-creative photographer is concerned, lies in the fact that he can convey and evoke feelings about things and situations and events which for some reason or other are not or can not be photographed. The secret, the catch and the power, lies in being able to use the forms and shapes of objects in front of the camera for their expressive-evocative qualities. Or to say this in another way, in practice Equivalency is the ability to use the visual world as the plastic material for the photographer's expressive purposes. He may wish to employ the recording power of the medium, it is strong in photography, and document. Or he may wish to emphasize its transforming power, which is equally strong, and cause the subject to stand for something else too. If he uses Equivalency consciously and knowingly, aware of what he is doing, and accepts the responsibility for his images, he has as much freedom of expression as [in] any of the arts.

The mechanisms by which a photograph functions as an Equivalent in a viewer's psyche are the familiar ones which the psychologists call "projection" and "empathy." In the art world the corresponding phenomenon is referred to as "expressive forms and shapes." In the world of photography the vast majority of viewers remain so subject-identification bound that they stay ignorant of the "expressive" qualities of shapes and forms or are unable to overcome their fear of letting themselves go and responding to "expressive" shapes or colors, that is, the design side of the pictorial experience. Yet fortunately, or unfortunately, as the case may be, the contemporary viewer of photographs nearly always responds subconsciously to the design embedded in photographs. This he can hardly help, as the world of advertising exploits constantly and expertly. The reader no doubt has heard of "hidden persuaders." If advertisers can use the subliminal effect of design in photography to help sell a product, a knowledgeable photographer can use the same aspect of design for more enlightened aesthetic purposes.

At a deeper level of Equivalence, the term refers to the specific effect of a photograph intended to function as an Equivalent. So far in this article it would seem that any awareness of mirroring on the part of the viewer looking at a photograph is related to Equivalence. Now we can revamp the definition somewhat to indicate that the feeling of Equivalence is specific. In literature this specific feeling associated with Equivalence is called "poetic," using this word in a very broad and universal sense. Not having an exact equivalent for the word "poetic" in photography, we will suggest the word "vision," meaning not only sight, but insight. The effect that seems to be associated with Equivalence may be worded thus: When both subject matter and manner of rendering are transcended, by whatever means, that which seems to be matter becomes what seems to be spirit.

A third level of Equivalence was mentioned earlier. This level revolves around the "remembered image." What a man remembers of vision is always peculiarly his own because various distortions occur and change his recall image after the original

stimulation has gone. These alterations from the original can only come from the individual himself. If a viewer happens to study in his mind a remembered image, who knows what degree or trajectory of Equivalence he might reach, or how far he might walk into his remembered image? The moment when a photograph transforms into a mirror that can be walked into, either when one is looking at it, or remembering it, must always remain secret because the experience is entirely within the individual. It is personal, his own private experience, ineffable, and untranslatable. People who report on this experience tell of literal transformations before their eyes, for example a picture that they know to be of peeled paint turns into something else.

To select this moment for which to make photographs hardly seems a likely area for productive camerawork, yet secret as

Frederick Sommer, *Arizona Landscape, 1945*

this moment is, a few photographers are working today who deliberately try to start from their own known feeling states to make photographs which will arouse or reach similar feeling states in others. They consciously make photographs to function as Equivalents. We can add the names of a few—Frederick Sommer, . . . Paul Caponigro, . . . Walter Chappell, . . . Gerald Robinson, . . . Arnold Gassan; . . . there are others.

To work in such a manner, the photographers must be able to get their work before those persons in the world who are sensitized intellectually, emotionally, and kinesthetically—not a numerous audience to be sure, even if widespread. Universality, that quality always thought to be desirable in photographs and pictures, is not denied to such photographers. It is their efforts that matter, to communicate-evoke with individuals who are in tune with the central core of universality common to both man and spirit.

From *PSA Journal* (Spring 1963), pp. 17–21.

Brett Weston, *Untitled*

My pictures speak only when we both listen. BRETT WESTON

William LaRue, *Untitled*

Aaron Siskind, *Martha's Vineyard III, 1954*

Let associations rise like a flock of birds from a field. What do various parts of the photograph remind you of—visually. What does the picture as a whole suggest, again visually.

MINOR WHITE, *Aperture*, 1959

Imogen Cunningham, *Magnolia Bud, 1925*

Dreams and photographs have something in common, those photographs that yield to contemplation at least have a quality about them that tempt one to set associations going.

What you will find will be your own. The experience cannot be compared to addition because that implies one right answer and many wrong ones. Instead the experience should be compared to an equation one factor of which is the viewer's depth mind. When so treated there are as many right answers as persons who contemplate the picture; and only one wrong answer— no experience.

MINOR WHITE, *Aperture*, 1959

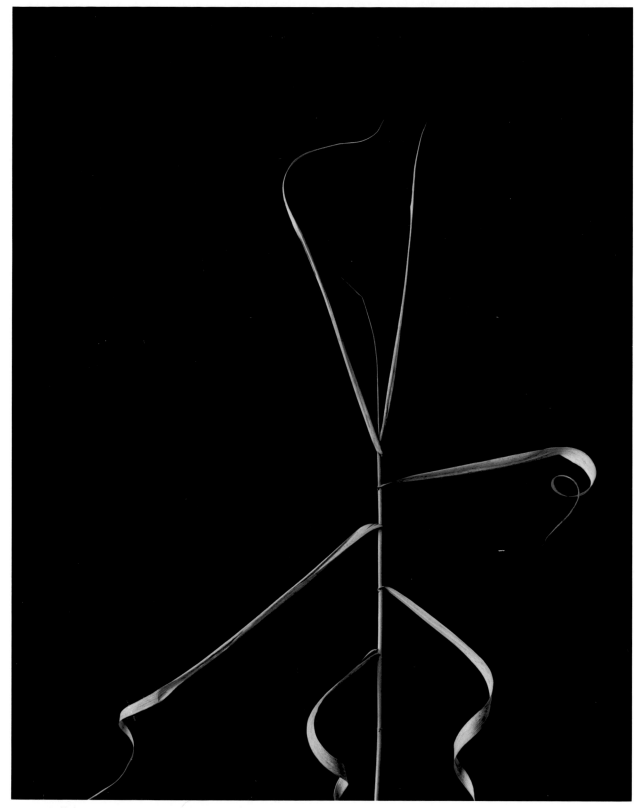

Harry Callahan, *Aix-en-Provence, 1958*

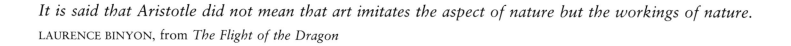

It is said that Aristotle did not mean that art imitates the aspect of nature but the workings of nature.
LAURENCE BINYON, from *The Flight of the Dragon*

The Threshold of Vision:
Minor White

WALTER CHAPPELL

I FIRST MET MINOR WHITE at Christmas, 1941, during a ten-day cross-country skiing trip sponsored by the Portland YMCA. There were fifteen of us staying in a lodge on the shore of Spirit Lake at Mount St. Helens, Washington. Each morning at dawn we rose, and after breakfast and packing lunches climbed the mountain on skis to descend swiftly by nightfall to the lodge for dinner by the roaring fireplace.

Minor caught my attention immediately and retained my respect throughout a lifelong friendship. We all arrived with our skiing and camping gear, and Minor with a wooden tripod and several leather cases of camera equipment. It was the first time I had seen a view camera at work anyplace, let alone on skis. Minor carried his camera and film holders, a 2¼ hand camera, and tripod up and down the slopes every day, taking many individual and group portraits of us that included intimate details of hands, boots, falling-down-in-the-snow gestures. During the evening as we ate and told stories around the fireplace in the soft light of kerosene lamps, he continued to photograph us. Being only sixteen, I was very impressed with this man of thirty-three who was doing everything we did plus the extra activity of observing, shooting, and exposing hundreds of pictures. Talking together more each day, Minor and I discovered our mutual interests in the visual arts, serious music, and psychological ideas opening doors into the metaphysical world of the human mind.

One evening Minor opened up a case of prints, which we passed around from hand to hand looking into eastern Oregon landscapes, portraits, Portland iron-front buildings, and street scenes along the waterfront. During the discussion that evening, he explained his intention to create a sequence from the selected results of all the prints from our trip and exhibit the work in the lobby of the Portland YMCA by spring.

Returning to town from this unusual journey, I was aware of a visual expansion within the familiar world of my regular life. I was attending two schools at that time—the Portland Conservatory of Music, which I had entered at age six on a scholarship, and a polytechnic school for boys where I majored in architectural drawing and building construction—and I was quite involved already with painting watercolors and oils on paper and canvas. As Minor had invited me to visit his darkroom to see the prints, I made my way to the third floor and knocked on the door that read "JANITOR." He opened the door and returned to the sink, where he was agitating prints. I had suddenly stepped into some other dimension.

We talked for some time as he turned the prints face up in the water, revealing faces, fir trees covered with snow, human gestures on and off skis, many unknown aspects in whiteness and lamplight of our common experiences. A string quartet played on the phonograph; as we talked Minor engaged in the continuous process of darkroom work—all of which seemed to me inevitably natural and complex. I returned the next day to see them in piles on a small table. We looked through them all several times over a few hours. I watched Minor building his first Spirit Lake sequence and saw a mode of communication develop.

The war erupted at Pearl Harbor, and ordinary life became turbulent. Minor vanished in the draft of April '42. I later saw an exhibition of his work at the Portland Art Museum, and a picture postcard showing the wreckage of Pearl Harbor arrived from him: a brief poem, cheerio, Minor. No return address. I registered, and vanished into the war on my eighteenth birthday as a voluntary paratrooper. Discharged in '46, I returned to Portland for a brief interval with the conservatory, and after a period of immense disorientation finally settled in San Francisco's North Beach, where I set up a studio and entered into a new period of painting and reintegration.

Within a few weeks after my arrival at the end of 1946 I encountered Minor in an alleyway leading from my place on Montgomery Street down into the old Produce Market area. As we approached, walking fast, I observed this man dressed in worn khaki clothes, with a baseball cap pulled close above the eyes, a hand camera hanging from his neck. We passed about ten steps and both of us turned around in great surprise to discuss everything all at once for an hour. He was sharing with students Ansel Adams's house near the Golden Gate Bridge, where he ate, slept, and worked in the darkroom. He wanted me to see a sequence he was making of his experience in the war: *Amputations.*

I went to his place early that evening, entering a well-tended garden filled with flowers and symphonic music emanating from one of two houses. Minor was there with a few students. Framed prints hung on the walls above many more standing on the floor. I was very happy to be there, to see this missed friend in his own atmosphere.

After the dinner table was cleared and the students had left, Minor carried to the table a large and heavy book, placed it in front of me, and left the room to change the music. I became absorbed working my way through the double pages of this powerful combination of images, writing, and psychic interplay. I looked through it twice during a timeless interval when I was allowed to acutely examine my own war of mutilations and begin to comprehend this man for what he could see as well as write:

> *If battle gives me time*
> *It is my will*
> *to cut away all dear insanities*
> *I get in War*
> *Or if I live*
> *To amputate the pain*
> *I've seen endured.*

I suddenly glanced across the room where he sat in a chair listening to the music and staring at me with a gaze I had never seen before. Coffee was made and we talked into the night about his studies in New York with Meyer Schapiro and the aesthetic theories of Wölfflin, then his experiences meeting Stieglitz and seeing prints of Edward Weston's. Minor clearly appraised the ideas surrounding the reality of Equivalency with a knowledge native to any artist working directly in the mediums of the visual arts, music, and metaphorical poetry. Minor had been very moved by Stieglitz's portrait series of Georgia O'Keeffe, and by Stieglitz asking if he had ever been in love. He had received a potent impression that he had to have this condensed emotion to engender an equivalent image in the medium of camerawork. He told me, "What I have to do is realize what Stieglitz told me. This is a simple thing, but a very difficult thing to understand."

We had exhausted the night when Minor showed me his writing room upstairs with a couch and blankets, where I would sleep. I left him setting prints out to dry and went to sleep. I was awakened by the smell of hot coffee and by sunlight streaming through a little window covered outside with delicate leaves like lace. Minor had to teach his class at the California Institute of Fine Arts. We raced toward North Beach in his topless jeep, stopping in front of a little house on Green Street, where he took me for the first of many meetings with his dear friend Imogen Cunningham. Later that afternoon he came to my studio to go through my paintings and drawings on our way to Chinatown for dinner, the first of countless Chinese meals and of countless discussions and exchanges of works, books, ideas, and support.

The first long field trip with Minor was to Big Sur for a large conference of Bay Area artists held over a three-day weekend at Slades Hot Springs (now Esalen). Here the most active creative people in California would gather to see experimental films and exhibitions and have discussions while soaking in hot tubs set into the cliff above the ocean. I drove with Minor. The long, windy drive brought us into the Sur after nightfall; we rolled out our sleeping bags in the grass, along with the hundred others who arrived through the night. The two-day program was extremely stimulating in a magnetic country where mountains bathe in the Pacific. I made a decision to return to this place as often as possible, and for several periods later in life I have lived there, always considering that country a sanctuary.

After stopping at Brett and Cole Weston's Garapata Ranch, where many photographers had migrated, we continued up the coast to the Point Lobos Preserve. Suddenly it was as if we were on a different planet. Minor became quietly serious, setting up the 4x5 on a tripod over his shoulder. I carried the bag of holders as we walked slowly through the ancient rock formations and tide pools in a state of profound incomprehension. We finally stopped near a well of jagged multicolored aggregate and he set up the view camera, asking me to help him make some portraits of me. While he directed me to slowly move

Walter Chappell, *Minor White Interior, 72 N. Union Street, Rochester, 1957*

around, sit, and lie down, he observed me intently, asking me direct personal questions regarding my life aims, my ideas relating to Taoism and the *I Ching*, and what sense of the Ineffable I may have ever been aware of. He insisted that I answer as he covered his head and the groundglass with the darkcloth, gazing and requestioning after each of my attempts to answer these essential inquiries.

The whole situation became totally extraordinary, lasting over an hour, during which he made six exposures, changing darkslides with a reassuring smile or a nod of the head. Then he became silent and lay on a slab of flat rocks in the sunshine facing the sky beyond the surf and gull flight. The sun was getting low as he looked about and shouldered his camera. We drove back all the way in silence. He showed me proofs a few days later but would not discuss them. They were pictures of someone I would come to know years later, in 1957 in Rochester, already wearing my clothing.

While painting watercolors on a pad on the slope of Telegraph Hill, under the shadow of Coit Tower, I met a woman my age just arrived from Utah. Jib and I became immediate companions, living together and collaborating in various mediums for the next six years. My first son was born through us. We soon moved my studio to New Monterey, above Cannery Row, and lived in Jean Vardas's Red Barn. We apprenticed in leatherwork and ceramics as I continued painting and made a living working nights in the sardine canneries. Minor had begun a series of weekend trips for his CSFA class to visit Edward Weston at his home at Wildcat Creek and photograph at nearby Point Lobos. He would usually drive down to stay with us the afternoon before and meet his students at Edward's the next day. Jib and I accompanied him on several visits at first, and I continued these trips for a period of months during 1947. Dody Warren was living with Weston as an apprentice, transcribing the *Daybooks* to reams of typewritten pages, which we all read. Weston's Paris show had just returned, allowing us hours of close examination of those superlative glass-encased prints.

Minor had the deepest respect for Weston, who was for him the living image of a spiritual father. In the evening, prints were laid out on the table for Edward to look over. He said very little, but his words were meaningful and direct when he saw what did not work. Minor brought his own prints along with his students' recent work. Many questions surfaced, but not many answers: just a nod of the head while Edward, sorting, left a few remaining prints in sight to look at. Parkinson seizures would pass through Weston's very present body. We would drive back to Monterey in silence.

Minor sometimes stayed over with us to photograph around the canneries and pursue the portrait quest. He would bring

Walter Chappell, *Picket Fence (#10), 1958*

prints down and take some paintings back, in order to see them in another place. I was painting more and more rapidly with egg tempera and inks on sheets of paper up to 5x8 feet. An enormity had been absorbed from my exposure to Minor and Weston. Jib had worked full hours at the cannery, saving money for a projected trip to Europe. At the last moment we bought an old station wagon, rolled up the paintings, and drove to New Orleans, where we lived for almost two years, with a trip to Cuba and Mexico. I obtained a Rolleiflex camera during that period and began an amateurish recycling of impressions through the drugstore. A long phase of correspondence with Minor began. When we returned to San Francisco he had already moved to the Jackson Street studio in North Beach.

In 1949 Ouspensky's original report of Gurdjieff's ideas about man's possible evolution had been published, which I began carefully studying in New Orleans. After we left Louisiana, the first edition of Gurdjieff's *All and Everything* was published, and I began reading it during the journey back to California and continued in Oregon and in Washington at Long Beach

and at Willapa Bay, where we built a studio onto a small cottage where I had lived my summers of childhood. We found Minor in a changed mode of life, very involved with teaching, writing, and working on a new sequence, *Intimations of Disaster*, which centered on his wide-scale vision of San Francisco. Seven new sequences were there to be studied in the new studio, and many days of quiet contemplation developed for me while beholding the remarkable transformations in his body of work. A few long night discussions exploring Gurdjieff's ideas had led us to a departure point; much more time would be involved at some other unknown interval. This was the interval when Minor had really come into his own work: he had mastered photography in his own singular way, crossing the gap beyond which there is no returning. He gave me *Sequence 4* to keep as we departed for Washington. I saw it as a map to infinity.

After several months of building and painting at Long Beach, it became imperative to contact Louise March in New York. Her address had been given to me in New Orleans by a musician who had attended readings from Gurdjieff that she had given for a group actively working on these ideas.

We arrived in San Francisco to find Minor in the midst of putting together the first issue of *Aperture* in March, 1952. I had never seen him so accelerated, certain of being in registration with Stieglitz and a rebirth of *Camera Work*. Jib and I hitchhiked cross country to New York during the first month of her pregnancy. We entered into the family life of Walter and Louise March under conditions of The Work. An immense alteration of consciousness occurred in me during seven months of directed physical efforts in an embryonic state of active meditation. In the midst of it all *Aperture #1* with a letter from Minor arrived in the mail. The first strong note in a new octave: Minor White and the destiny of Creative Photography.

With this omen we packed up and drove back to Long Beach in time for Sharma Chakravarty to be born where he had been conceived. Within a few months I was back in San Francisco opening a shop in North Beach with Yone Aroshiro, an artist who had studied with Morris Graves. Like-minded people began to gravitate to this activity, and a group was formed to study the ideas that made work on oneself possible. Minor visited this new activity but remained shy of direct involvement. He was ever open to talking these matters over in the privacy of his or my own studio when time allowed. These impressions were salted away to emerge again in Rochester in the 1957–63 period. I soon opened a studio-gallery in the upper Fillmore, exhibiting the large panel version of *Sequence 8, Intimations of Disaster* with single prints of recent portraits-of-people-becoming, along with my large batik panels and paintings.

Minor came to the opening with some of his students. He had a role to play with teaching that both conflicted and otherwise ran parallel with his solitary work as an artist. Teaching activated him. It allowed him to work through the barriers of approval/disapproval that fetter us all and became a personal dialogue in which the students' minds filled the void of any sexual-family interior exploration. By knowing Weston in actual life-process he could understand more of Stieglitz. Teaching became the crystallization of his thought as a writer/editor when catalyzed by his personal work as a highly original artist. However, the real tuition was being himself, performing a definite line of development that nurtured his body of work. In this way I know I studied with him all the time I knew him. Teaching was as necessary to him as to those he attracted by a special atmospheric activity. He was attempting to discover through his work, students, and friends a faculty of vision that seemed to be present only during moments of active realization: how could one retain these insights, prolong them, fuse them with the instantaneous nature of the photographic image? These were questions that challenged us to search for verifications through a growth of efforts to *see intentionally*.

The practice of throwing an *I Ching* hexagram allowed a simple discipline directing the attention needed to develop a field of awareness. Even though the lines that build the trigrams into images are abstract and primitive, they structure meaning enough to arouse visualization from the interior. A coincidence of meaning may take place as one goes out into the chaos of the world, when suddenly an interior image registers in fusion with events. The exterior is a reflection of the interior, not the other way around. These ideas were resonant with what Minor was doing and became more important as his life continued to change.

Just before Minor left to join the staff of George Eastman House, he installed a special exhibition at the San Francisco Museum of Art, "How to Read a Photograph," which was a cogent summation of his camerawork and demonstrated conclusions he had reached upon the termination of the CSFA teaching program. A group of us—painters, craftspeople, musicians, poets—attended the exhibit several different days. We all noticed, when leaving the museum to walk through the city, how everything we were seeing was transformed by his sensibility instilled within and demonstrated by the pictures. The threshold of vision had been entered by all of us. It was the dissemination of an essential vision that is direct teaching. Minor developed *Aperture* into a vehicle for this search. He left San Francisco inspired by the new turn his life was taking, and I did not see him again until I arrived in Rochester in the early spring of 1957.

I had moved to Big Sur to recover from an illness induced by inhaling beeswax and solvent fumes while batik-making. I lived with a few friends at Anderson Creek, where we worked together in preparation for entering an opening of a Group for Special Studies at Taliesin West, in the desert north of Scottsdale, Arizona. During a year of unusual and intensive work there, I encountered the metamorphosis of my life that hospitalized me for three years in Denver, where all of my creative interests suddenly fused with the medium of photography.

Arnold Gassan, whom I had met in New Orleans, was living in Denver and related to the small intellectual world isolated there. He immediately introduced me to Winter Prather, a good working photographer who had just returned from Yosemite, where he had attended Ansel Adams's workshop. Nile Root operated a camera shop and rental darkroom next door to the hospital. It was here where a 4x5 Graflex with 9″ Dagor lens became mine for $75. Winter offered me a short-term apprenticeship in field and darkroom work. Gassan began his photography then, making many field trips possible. The Zone System became our master. Correspondence with Minor during this period was more encouraging, and he sent along fresh issues of *Aperture*, along with *Image* newsletters from Eastman House, which he also edited.

My concentration on camerawork very soon eclipsed long practice in painting and drawing. Once I could begin to grasp

Minor White, *Walter Chappell, 72 N. Union Street, Rochester, 1957*

the technical problems as tools, my vision as a painter rapidly moved from linear confines into the strangely natural domain where simultaneity is actualized. Winter modified my Graflex into an instrument that worked like a 4x5 Hasselblad, based on his 1000F hand camera. It was the only camera I used until 1958, when I obtained a Linhoff, which allowed much more dexterity of motion in the lens axis and focal plane. Photography had changed and clarified my life, precipitating a complete recovery and release from the hospital.

I had intended to return to work at Taliesin, but, encouraged by Minor's letter and urgent invitation to visit him and see Eastman House, I packed up. I arrived on the doorstep of 72 North Union Street shivering in the last snow at the edge of spring. Minor opened the door with a long look turning into an immense embrace before we climbed up the wood staircase tunneling to his large second-floor flat. Upon entering this spacious atmosphere, I sensed the actuality of my footprints standing between the parallels of the known and the unknown.

Walter Chappell, *City of Rocks, Southern New Mexico, 1981*

The idea of equivalence is an equation that is all at once. It takes in the entire mind. Everything works for a moment. The blessing of the photographic image is the precision involved. There is no chance, except the chance that there is an intelligent being who will press the shutter at the moment of the equation. Then the image stays as a cogent emblem of eternity. Photography allows you to do that. It insists that you be there.

WALTER CHAPPELL

Walter Chappell, *Hands, Dorset Sheep Skull, William Gratwick's Estate, Pavilion, New York, 1957*

Photograph to remember what you have not yet seen.   WALTER CHAPPELL

Frederick Sommer, *Untitled Landscape, 1947*

Frederick Sommer, *Smoked Glass, 1964*

WE NEVER GO to strange places. Maybe the fare is expensive, and so, after some kind of expensive travel, we think we're in exotic country. But, if we are somewhat comfortable there, it's because we took a chunk of ourselves and found something of ourselves again. There is nothing at all to *East shall never meet West*. The world is not a world of cleavages at all; the world is a world of bonds. Circulation of the blood is always cicumnavigation of the world.

What appears to be a new, exciting condition you recognize as such because it is alive to you already and a great part of you. You find a chance to let your feelings grow and enrich themselves in this new condition; you're basking in a new country. But you bask in this new country because you are already there.

I have seen more and more the reasons why I have been using photography as a funnel to a final condition. I say *final* in a tentative way. I'm interested in sensitized surfaces. In an age where sense perception is the thing that is either making us all or killing us all, we are obsessed with it in one way or another. We favor situations and relationships that enable us, through sensitized conditions, to play on ourselves as instruments. Since we are involved in many ways in instrumentation, why not carry this instrumentation onto the final surface?

FREDERICK SOMMER

Frederick Sommer, *Venus, Jupiter, and Mars, 1949*

Minor in La Grande, 1940–1941

ISABEL KANE BRADLEY

THE YEARS IN LA GRANDE, Oregon, were very important to Minor's whole perspective and life. It was the first time to my knowledge that he had been to the West. La Grande was a town of about eight thousand people, in the middle of nowhere and about fifty miles from the next town. It was surrounded by wheat fields and wilderness. In the spring of 1940 Minor

Isabel Kane Bradley, *Minor in La Grande, 1939–41*

arrived to set up an arts center with WPA funds. He was absolutely wide-eyed at this great country.

This was an extraordinary time for Minor. He was free to develop his talents in a very wild and primitive area with no other artist of note around him. He was entirely the source of his own creativity. We were in La Grande together for about

two and a half years. I was head of the Physical Education Department of Eastern Oregon College, and I attended Minor's photography class. We would take rides and he would see a view and we would return as many as three or four times to get the right light or the right angle. There is one photograph of a plowed field, with the rows going this way and that, that required many trips to get the right light. He photographed many barn doors. Just a few miles out of La Grande was the Grand Ronde Valley where a number of his photographs were taken. Time meant nothing. He had no responsibility other than the arts center, and my car and I were at his disposal.

Living in such a town, one is totally isolated. We were happy with each other and not too aware of what was going on in the war. In the spring of 1941 I had a week's vacation and Minor wanted to explore the mountains. We rode horses and used a pack horse for our gear and set out like babes in the wood. Minor showed no signs of knowing anything about the wilderness. We spent the week in the Wallowa Mountains. There were a beautiful lake, mountain flowers, and driftwood that had been there for centuries. (This was country where no one had set foot.) We set up camp, cooked, explored, swam in the little mountain lakes, and had a beautiful time.

We were like brother and sister. I liked the outdoors, and he was ecstatic. But the war was getting closer and there was this talk of the draft. Minor was thirty-two and unmarried. He said that when the draft came he wouldn't have a leg to stand on. He began to become depressed. Once along a country road we passed a squirrel that had been run over by a truck. I stopped the car for him and he leaned over the dead squirrel to photograph it. "This is what the war means. That smashed animal just got caught. There is no rhyme or reason for it."

The arts-center funds started to drop off. Soon the center folded and Minor went to Portland and got a job in a department store playing Santa Claus, a role that describes him. He was somebody interested in everything yet detached. By this time I was teaching in central Washington. We hadn't seen each other since the fall. His sudden letter arrived saying that his draft notice had come. I was beside myself. We both had the weekend so I drove to Portland to meet him. We just drove to the ocean. We went automatically. I don't know what the town was called, but we found a cabin with a stove in it. It was a full moon and we spent that night together. He told me about his childhood

Minor White, *Grande Ronde Valley from Mt. Emily, 1941*

and his feelings on marriage, an idea he didn't entirely rule out, though he never saw himself as a family man.

Within a matter of days he was on a boat going out for training in the Pacific. Thrown in with thousands of other draftees he was piled on as a private. He didn't know what hit him.

Just before the end of the war when the boys in Europe were getting ready to go to Japan, he wrote me in Paris. He said that as soon as the war ended he was going to give his life to photography.

From an interview by Christopher Cox

My approach to photography at that time, first recognized during 1940 in La Grande, Oregon, was more or less as follows: "Surfaces reveal inner states—cameras record surfaces. Confronted with the world of surfaces in nature, man, and photographs, I must somehow be a kind of microscope by which the underlying forces of spirit are observed and extended to others."

MINOR WHITE, from *Mirrors, Messages, Manifestations,* 1969

Edward Weston, *Hat and Shoes, 1926*

Artists (fine ones) don't copy nature, and when they do record quite literally the presentation is such as to arouse connotations quite apart from the subject matter.

EDWARD WESTON, from *My Camera on Point Lobos*

Barbara Morgan, *Minor White in Edward Weston's studio,*
Pt. Lobos, ca. 1950

A TEACHING JOB at the California School of Fine Arts became available. The Newhalls recommended me to Ansel Adams
and I appeared in San Francisco on my birthday, 1946. Home
at last.

All the background of science, art, teaching, photographing,
living with people, writing, traveling, was suddenly channeled
into teaching at CSFA. I felt that I did not know enough.

Barbara Morgan, *Edward Weston,*
Pt. Lobos, ca. 1950

The lessons learned from Boleslavsky went into effect. The
principles of art history were converted to use by photographers;
the psychological approach learned from Schapiro went into
effect, the idea of the equivalent from Stieglitz went into the
curriculum; technique was learned from Ansel at a high rate of
speed and his Zone System became my staple.

"Memorable Fancies," 1945-1946

Time off and away to Edward Weston and Point Lobos! [On
the first visit for the group it] rained hard. When it let up Edward
took us to the Point. He told us to leave our cameras behind.
He was right, we wouldn't have gone twenty yards.

We saw the cliffs and ocean meet at Lobos with Edward's
own eyes: rich, magnificent, wet with magic. The low sun broke
a cloud—magic nee gold this time (sic). The second part of the
tour to the beaches made me impatient; beautiful, but I was
powerfully drawn to the North Shore and I hurried back and
used up a dozen sheets of film.

Barbara Morgan, *Edward Weston, Pt. Lobos, ca.* 1950

Dinner and the spotlighted pictures in the evening. I had not
seen [Edward] since the retrospective at The Museum of Modern
Art. All the next day initials appeared on the ground glass, EW.
And the work started to find my own Lobos. Edward was
always helpful; "I have scratched the surface of Lobos. Make
your own scratch."

Lobos never looked this way again to me. And I do not think
this was entirely due to my search for my own but because
Edward's decline had started, a sympatico between man and
place dwindled. As he waned so did Lobos.

"Memorable Fancies," December 1946

Ansel Adams, *Roots, Foster Gardens, Honolulu, 1948*

MY LAST MEMORY OF MINOR is a lecture he gave in Tucson, Arizona, shortly before his passing. His lecture provided an unusually clear and exciting perspective not only into photography but also into a very particular aspect of life itself. Minor closed with a series of 35mm color slides of beach-sand details—delicate, immensely varied, yet all comprising a prayer-like devotion to that rare component of our time: beauty. The slides were shown in silence, and I could sense the firm bond of attention of the large audience. Then the lights went on, Minor moved casually before the screen to say "Thank you very much," and that was all. Once again he had created an important experience for people—one of the best I ever witnessed.

Minor believed, he dreamed, he visualized, and he generously communicated with his students and colleagues. His craft was superb, and the cohesion of craft with creativity in his work and teaching is a monumental contribution to the art of photography—and to all arts. I feel that we are now in a stage of external mechanistic marvels and internal spiritual desolation. But in time to come I am sure we will regain this comprehension of unity of purpose of art and craft that distinguished Minor's work. His photographs will be like a golden thread between ages of darkness and light.

I met Minor in 1946 when he came to San Francisco to teach at the California School of Fine Arts (now the San Francisco Institute of Art). Naturally I can recall many anecdotes and stories, but such episodes are rather shallow in comparison to the excursions that Minor led into the profound world of spirit. CSFA provided the opportunity for Minor to enhance his craft through the experience of teaching, a continuing experience through the years to come. For him, fine craft was essential to the creation of art in any form—a message of increasing validity in our confused and materialistic times. He always stressed the revelation of self, and in his photographs we find assured reason to believe in beauty, confidence, and enlightenment—surely one of the great achievements of any work of art at any time.

I am grateful that Minor White was my friend and am humbled by the opportunity he gave me to observe genius in its most compelling form.

ANSEL ADAMS

Ansel Adams, *Clouds Above Golden Canyon, Death Valley, California, 1945*

Barbara Morgan, *Pure Energy and Neurotic Man, 1940*

I WAS GIVING A LECTURE in Cambridge on photography and had learned that he was not well. I went to his house. There were several people taking care of him. One of them escorted me upstairs to his bedroom. I opened the door and walked in. The moment I walked in he recognized me. I impulsively started to hug him and he impulsively started to put his arms around me, but his arms were bones, he was already almost gone. It was so eerie to feel that he was hardly alive, but these skinny bones went around my neck. He was half dead. It was the most shocking, traumatic experience I can ever remember. So we hugged each other, then he made a few jokes, typically. It was so intense that I almost fainted. I went out of there in a state. I thought: his body is gone but his soul will never go. Who knows about theories of afterlife? But it made me think there may be life after death. He was very much spiritually alive yet he was nothing but bones. His spirit was so intense. He was smiling.

BARBARA MORGAN

Barbara Morgan, *Pearl Primus, Speak to Me of Rivers, 1944*

Barbara Morgan, *Emergence, 1979*

CONTEMPLATION, then, in the most general sense is a power which we may—and often must—apply to the perception, not only of Divine Reality, but of anything. It is a mental attitude under which all things give up to us the secret of their life. All artists are of necessity in some measure contemplative. In so far as they surrender themselves without selfish preoccupation, they see Creation from the point of view of God. "Innocence of eye" is little else than this: and only by its means can they see truly those things which they desire to show the world. I invite those to whom these statements seem a compound of cheap psychology and cheaper metaphysics to clear their minds and submit this matter to an experimental test. If they will be patient and honest—and unless they belong to that minority which is temperamentally incapable of the simplest contemplative act—they will emerge from the experiment possessed of a little new Knowledge as to the nature of the relation between the human mind and the outer world.

All that is asked is that we shall look for a little time, in a special and undivided manner, at some simple, concrete, and external thing. This object of our contemplation may be almost anything we please: a picture, a statue, a tree, a distant hillside, a growing plant, running water, little living things. We need not, with Kant, go to the starry heavens. "A little thing the quantity of a hazel nut" will do for us, as it did for Lady Julian long ago. Remember it is a practical experiment on which we are set: not an opportunity of pretty and pantheistic meditation.

Look, then, at this thing which you have chosen. Willfully, yet tranquilly, refuse the messages which countless other aspects of the world are sending; and so concentrate your whole attention on this one act of loving sight that all other objects are excluded from your conscious field. Do not think, but, as it were, pour out your personality towards it: let your soul be your eyes. Almost at once, this new method of perception will reveal unsuspected qualities in the external world. First you will perceive about you a strange and deepening quietness; a slowing down of our feverish mental time. Next you will become aware of a heightened significance, an intensified existence in the thing at which you look.

As you, with all your consciousness, lean out towards it, an answering current will meet yours. It seems as though the barrier between its life and your own, between subject and object, had melted away. You are merged with it, in an act of true communion: and *you* know the secret of its being, deeply and unforgettably, yet in a way which you can never hope to express.

Seen thus, a thistle has celestial qualities: a speckled hen a touch of the sublime. . . . Life has spoken to life, but not to the surface intelligence. That surface intelligence knows only that the message was true and beautiful: no more.

I do not suggest that this simple experiment is in any sense to be equated with the transcendental contemplation of the mystic. Yet it exercises on a small scale, and in regard to visible Nature, the same natural faculties which are taken up and used by the mystic. Though it is one thing to see truthfully for an instant the flower in the crannied wall, and another to be lifted up to the appreciation of "eternal Truth, true Love, and loved Eternity," yet both according to their measure are functions of the inward eye, operating in the "suspension of the mind."

EVELYN UNDERHILL, from *Mysticism*

Charles Arnold, *Eastman House Garage, Rochester, ca. 1956*

To show the moment to itself
Is to liberate the moment.

ALFRED STIEGLITZ

David Horton, *The Abandoned Star Factory, 1979*

THE STATE OF MIND of the photographer while creating is a blank. I might add that this condition exists only at special times, namely when looking for pictures. . . . For those who would equate "blank" with a kind of static emptiness, I must explain that this is a special kind of blank. It is a very active state of mind really, a very receptive state of mind, ready at an instant to grasp an image, yet with no image pre-formed in it at any time. We should note that lack of a pre-formed pattern or preconceived idea of how anything ought to look is essential to this blank condition. Such a state of mind is not unlike a sheet of film itself—seemingly inert, yet so sensitive that a fraction of a second's exposure conceives a life in it.

The photographer projects himself into everything he sees, identifying himself with everything in order to know it and feel it better. To reach such a blank state of mind requires effort, perhaps discipline. Out of such a state of mind he loves much, hates much, and is aware of the areas of his indifference. He photographs what he loves because he loves it, what he hates out of protest; the indifferent he can pass over or photograph with whatever craftsmanship of technique and composition he commands.

"Blank" as the creative photographer's mind is, uncritical as it is while photographing, as sensitized, as prepared for anything to happen, afterwards with the prints safely in hand he needs to practice the most conscious criticism. Is what he saw present in the photograph? If not, does the photograph open his eyes to something he could not see by himself? If so, will he take responsibility for the accident and show it as his own, or will he consider it as a sketch for his subconscious to digest? He needs to study further the reactions of the viewers: do they match his own? come close? or depart in amazing directions? In a sense this is the activity that brings the creative state of mind near the boiling point: conscious criticism of new prints, digestion of what the prints do, as compared to what he wanted them to do. Without this siege of analytical work, the state of sympathetic sensitivity, the "blank" state of mind, will not recur.

MINOR WHITE, from "The Camera Mind and Eye," 1952

WHEN A PHOTOGRAPH IS BORN of a creative experience it gives nourishment. It is thus that the viewer, nourished by the work of art, is associated with the creative. At such moments a poem, a new photograph, or any serious effort is a rebirth. In this can be found our way of contemplating, of touching, immortality.
NICHOLAS HLOBECZY

Nicholas Hlobeczy, *Meditation Room, 1975*

Minor White As Teacher

Minor White, *Self Portrait, 72 N. Union Street, Rochester, 1958*

IN HIS WORK with the students in his illustration class at Rochester Institute of Technology, and in his workshops which had become annual affairs in Oregon, Minor continued to develop the ideas implicit in the Zen relationship (suggested in Eugen Herrigel's *Zen in the Art of Archery* or in the writings of Chuang Tsu, in the rich, evocative source of the *I Ching,* which both he and Walter Chappell had consulted for years, and now in the new relationship with the Gurdjieff workshop group in Rochester. It was sometime in the early 1960s that Minor began commuting to New York City to work with William Nyland.

Writing in a letter in September 1961 he commented regarding his own pace and work that, "Working from the 3rd of September to the 15th entirely alone put me wise to a few facts about myself. For one, that I keep busy in order to keep from working on myself. So with that discovery I can direct my work towards remembering myself." This last phrase is a Gurdjieffian nomenclature in which the act of self-discovery, or "remembering," which is a moment in which conscious attention is focused on oneself, was to be a principal tool in one's personal dedication to a personal realization. This was—in the language of the group—impossible without a series of outside assistances. Without shocks, specific stresses that would cause momentary destructions of the crystallization of the personality, rebuilding of oneself in a conscious way was impossible. Such shocks could happen from life, but best happened when they were directed.

In a letter in October 1961 he remarked on another teaching tool. He wrote that he had "re-encountered hypnotism, and again my respect increases while my suspicion does not. But this time I located a point in the teaching process where it might seem beneficial."

He briefly described using hypnotism to permit a quick change from black and white vision to color vision: "hypnotism suggests other possibilities to me in getting people to learn how to concentrate. Hypnosis has some kind of a bearing on being still with one's self and working on the self."

ARNOLD GASSAN, from
A Personal Legacy

IN A WORKSHOP, Minor would place a covered print on an easel and would tell the group to stare at the print, concentrate on it, think of nothing else. The room would be darkened, the easel would be lighted. "Take everything out of your mind and look only at that covered print." That is the initial basis for inducing a trance state—to fix your attention on one subject. Then he would take off the cover of the print and say, "Now look at the print, see nothing else but the print, concentrate on it, understand what it means, focus on the elements of the print, pay no attention to anything else in the room." This too is a hypnotic technique, because in hypnosis a person is required to focus on an object, to eliminate all extraneous noises and stimuli and to focus completely; only then is the person suggestible. His next step would be to ask questions: "What do you see? What do you feel about that print? Where does it strike you? Do you feel it in your muscles? Do you feel it in your bones? What is it doing to your head?" People would begin to respond to the print. Frequently the responses to the print would be totally different than if it had been viewed on an exhibition wall. Minor became very encouraged by this technique, because he believed he could get beyond the surface image of the print into the deeper meanings of what the photographer was trying to convey. There were hypnotic techniques to get you into that state of heightened awareness.

In 1963, Portland was a center for the study of hypnotherapy. One day I hosted a meeting of The International Society of Experimental Hypnosis and invited Minor. I said to those in attendance: "You are interested in seeing what new principles can be evoked with hypnosis. Here is Minor White, who is a photographer. I think he has something to offer using hypnotic technique." Minor put up a print, and several distinguished people from Australia, Canada, Germany, and the Orient looked at it. At the end of a three-hour session, they agreed that Minor had indeed evolved a hypnotic technique for interpreting photographs.

DR. ARNOLD RUSTIN,
interviewed by James Enyeart, 1978

Andrew de Lory, *Minor White, Undated*

IN 1957 my photography came to an impasse. I sent for an application from Rochester Institute of Technology. With what little courage I had left to continue as a photographer I went up to Rochester to sharpen my eye and technique.

It was really a fluid time for photography. "Everyone seems to be in Rochester," Dorothea Lange told me when I asked to be an apprentice with her the year before. Beaumont and Nancy Newhall had come to Rochester to direct George Eastman House. Nathan Lyons had just got out of the Air Force and had moved to Rochester with his family. Ralph Hattersley was "discovering himself" through photography at Rochester Institute of Technology and was asking

his unsuspecting students "to examine the unexamined life." Hollis Todd, on the other hand, an absolutely inspiring science teacher, was swinging pieces of chalk in the air, describing electrons, wavelengths, and the nature of light. Walter Chappell was stalking around. Jerry Uelsmann, Bruce Davidson, Peter Bunnell, David Plowden, Paul Caponigro, Pete Turner were all around being catalyzed and contributing to this flow of communication. It was a golden age. There were no labels to separate the serious playfulness of the game. Minor was in his element.

I first met Minor White at Eastman House. He was crouched on the floor amid hundreds of photographs, assem-

bling a massive sequence of about a hundred and fifty photographs along with words into what he called Sequence 13—*Return to the Bud*. This was hung in 1959 at Eastman House. He viewed this show as a retrospective of all the work he had done in the past, all his writings, and all that he had learned about layout through the various issues of *Aperture* and *Image* for which he had been responsible. All focused it into a single statement. He then adhered his words and photographs on large painted panels that stretched a couple of hundred feet like a continuous unfolding Chinese scroll as they wandered into four spaces. He was speaking about "the utter and sheer sentimentality" of Steichen's *Family of Man* show.

Knowing Minor at that time was also an introduction to his vision. He was always very open about it, and more than willing to share everything he knew with anyone who was not too threatening to him. He showed his love for Edward Weston's work and the simplicity that he was striving for. He introduced me to Nancy Newhall, so I could read the as yet unpublished *Daybooks* over at her house. And then he swept me into Paul Strand's vast vision and the lyrical objectivity with which he "could see right through his people to their very essence." He shared with me his deep respect and admiration for Ansel Adams's work, and the "miracles this man could produce with light." But the person with whom he identified most strongly was Alfred Stieglitz. It perplexed him deeply that he didn't seem to have Stieglitz's charisma to attract the kind of personalities he did. He felt he was indeed following Stieglitz's way, and often compared the spirit of *Camera Work* to his own *Aperture*. He wanted to give form to a universal language brought together by the best visionary minds in the world, and create through *Aperture* an open forum.

WILLIAM GILES

George Peet, *Minor White, Undated*

IT IS DIFFICULT to overestimate the impact of Minor's first Oregon workshop on the photographers who participated in it. There was a very rigorous routine each of the ten days of the workshop. We met at about seven in the morning. Minor would talk on some facet of photography

WHEN I MET Minor, he was in his early sixties. My remembered impression of him is of a tall, unassuming man, with a white mane of hair sitting back on a large forehead.

I had been recommended by a dancer friend to take her place assisting him in his Creative Audience classes at MIT.

He described his purpose for incorporating movement into his classes: "We are trying to escape from just thinking. One of the fastest ways to do it is to use body movement. It is one way of sharing our experience, and through sharing, to deepen our understanding."

We stood by the door of his office right before my first session. "I'm not going to tell you what to do. That's up to you. But you'll hear from me if what you do is wrong," he said with precision, in a deep resonant voice punctuated with even deeper throat clearing. Then we went in to class.

After class, I heard from him! He was anything but unassuming. With one eyebrow raised over a piercing eye, he elongated his face and boomed at me. "Never use the word 'heavy' when you are guiding a relaxation. They must visualize light! Light is weightless."

"But I used 'heavy' in contrast to feeling light weight. If you feel heavy deeply enough, you become light . . . ," I responded quickly, protecting myself, offering motive.

He explained that heavy is comparable to dark. Contractive and restrictive. "Light is expansive. Illuminating. Choose your images carefully to get the results you want," he said, shaking my hand.

"I'm sure this is the beginning of a long association." It was—and the association continues.

During the seven years that followed, I assisted him in many Creative Audience sessions. They were to influence my way of life and change my future work. Students and colleagues came and went. His work was a passageway to new lands. For many, it changed their direction. Some were with him only for a moment, others remained.

He coached and coaxed, inspired and challenged. He shook apart rigid responses. "I make the waves," he said, as I struggled with a resistance. "You must ride them."

I found his approach so valuable I be-

gan sharing it with artists in other fields. Many were starved for feedback that went beyond likes and dislikes. Through the years I have seen musicians, painters, actors, writers, and others find nourishment and renewal from developing their own small "creative audiences." All modified the exercises according to the needs of their art form, enlarging the approach with others from their field. Minor's work lives on through many extensions.

I have often been asked what was the structure of a Creative Audience session? I can only touch on it here, offer a brief outline and some of the philosophy.

The sessions usually began with music. As people entered, they would be asked to sit quietly and listen, or move freely around the room, interpreting. The guided-movement period followed. Mi-

and then give us assignments, which some would try to fulfill. When we felt that we had finished, we would adjourn—this was always around eleven or twelve o'clock—go back home, develop the film, make prints, mount them. In an evening session Minor would give a critique of the work that was done during the day.

The result of this routine was a growing exhaustion on the part of the students, though Minor was careful to nap in the afternoons. It was just this effect of exhaustion that Minor counted on to break down our resistance to new ideas, for he advanced several concepts that affected many of us deeply and changed not only our photography but our lives. One of them was expressed in a postcard from Minor to me dated April 23, 1961: "Memorable Fancy—When a photograph mirrors a man, and the man mirrors the world, it becomes possible that both can fuse into a mirror of Spirit."

For many of us who had photographed for quite a while, this kind of mental transformation was not particularly difficult, and it was helpful to explore what concentration in a formal and carefully managed way would yield in serious photography. It was also interesting to apply the principle of concentration to the examination of both our prints and those of other photographers. He taught us how to systematically read a print and to develop heightened awareness of its contents, not only the formal relationships of shapes, details, tonal values, and composition but also the emotional and symbolic content.

GERALD ROBINSON

nor depended upon movement work to prepare for working with images in a "seeing state": He explained: "Movement can be used for making contact with the livingness of a subject. When we look at something with attention, its energy flow affects our energy flow. When our awareness is increased, our energy goes out to that which we embrace with our attention. It shapes that energy and returns it to us in a new form. Discovering how our energy is shaped by our environment is the key to understanding our relationship to it."

The movement was followed by a period of "looking at photographs." Minor would guide us carefully through steps for conscious viewing and sharing responses, aimed at developing our ability to induce and work in a state of seeing.

It began with a preparation time for

choosing an image and consciously relaxing, then moved to making contact with the image in a state of heightened awareness. A longer time was given to exploring every element in the photograph and setting up resonance with the whole. He then emphasized the period of leaving the image, turning off. The next was a sharing of our responses, a period of communication.

During my portion of classes with new students, I could usually see a look of "what does this have to do with photography?" on most of their faces. In the early years, I braced myself against their reaction, which usually led to resistance to movement. Later, I would smile to myself. I knew Minor's goal: movement work

removed resistances, physical and psychological.

Minor wrote two companion manuscripts, "The Expressive Photographer" and "Creative Audience." In the first, he wrote, "The exercises for consciousness in photography, or camerawork, start with the individual's need to express, then move towards his maturing needs to communicate and finally to share with others his inner environment." Minor's career moved in this way also.

"Become aware of where an image is contacting you. Maintain that awareness as the shutter is being released. Be conscious of it and you, and the resonance between you."

Minor and I shared a "gesture." It burst forth one workshop day, like an excited child's bubble. It continued through the years and, by its repetition, became a kind of symbol for our relationship. One day he grabbed my hands, which were prayerlike in front of me, placing his around them in the same position. He spoke of his vision for photography, for what he thought his workshops could awaken in people's lives. He had just experienced a photograph that was to him a segment of life that contained and spoke of the whole.

"The image is complete . . . and asks no questions." He was uplifted, joyful. "This is what I want others to see. This is a metaphor for the whole. Not a seeking, but a celebration!"

I stood there for the longest time incorporating his experience.

The next time he reached out, I sensed it at the impulse stage (well trained as a

creative audience). My impulse was to do the same. We always seemed, from then on, to end with laughter as his hands clasped the air and mine clasped his.

Many gathered for a meeting at his home in Arlington, Massachusetts, the last year of his life. He had been near death and had come back.

We met in his hallway. The clasping of hands came spontaneously. He spoke excitedly of his future years of teaching, of joining together in the fall to work on a new manuscript of "Creative Audience." His old manuscript was outdated, he said. He'd learned so much while lying there in the hospital!

I hardly heard what he was saying, I was so moved by a sensation spreading through his hands to me. His hands scarcely felt human; they were so light I could barely feel substance. He seemed filled with light. Expansive. Less than a month later, he died.

SHIRLEY PAUKULIS

I THINK THAT if Minor gave us something that was more important than anything else, it was a language to deal with photographs. The usual language, "I like this" or "I don't like this," was eliminated. "This is too dark or too light" or "Here are the highlights"—that we eliminated too. Now we had to deal with the purpose of the photographer. "How did I feel this print?" "What emotions did it arouse in me?" "Was it successful in the sense that it brought something forth for me?" So we employed a new language in dealing with photographs.

DR. ARNOLD RUSTIN

Thomas Schuler, *Minor White, Undated*

MINOR WHITE'S WORKSHOP, a seminar on anthropomorphism, was offered at George Eastman House in the winter of 1953–54. None of us had heard of Minor White, and we were unprepared for his investment of the term with such elaborate iconography. Objects we had formerly isolated by their literal functions became subject matter for abstract experiments in photography. Minor's associational responses to photographs stimulated our vision until things became what they reminded us of. We accepted these analogies and exhausted our limited experience; feeling and curiosity had moved us past our knowledge. It was the first time most of us had reached the frontier of our sophistication and seen the need for inner development in order to read pictures better. Content ceased being a review of craft; technique was something in which the hard work of looking at photographs conceptually was central to creating stronger ones.

Minor taught the photojournalism major in the fall of 1955 at Rochester Institute of Technology. It was a much less unlikely choice than it appears: picture sequencing, exhibition design, and the relationship of words to images were all part of his personal work. The first assignment he gave us was one he called "the shotgun method." We had to shoot 1000 negatives at the Farmers' Market without any research. Simply be there at 2 A.M., stay until that evening, and record everything—early arrivals, setting up, shopping, the local diner, and the close of business. Some romanticized the subject, found the strange, while others saw a plain, hard struggle. But to all of us the shifts of emphasis that came from changing a picture's context brought with them a new visual syntax.

We were sent there to collect information without knowing its eventual use. Later, editing would supply the structure, defining character and action. We had assumed that photography returned the external world to the viewer as a familiar, portable artifact rather than a description of facts realigned by individual history. The reading of photographs, with its reliance on psychology, revealed a paradox: the medium's dependency on physical reality opened out into the imagination; art measured meaning in direct relationship to appearances and operated too fast to trust to memory or intent.

Minor White went out to the California School of Fine Arts during the summer of 1956 to run a workshop. It was my first opportunity to see him removed from RIT and with older people, many of whom were friends and former students. It was more of a party than a class. They challenged him repeatedly. Martin Baer, a painter in his seventies who had been a successful surrealist and shown in the thirties at The Museum of Modern Art, stood up and shouted, "Photography is a democratic medium and it belongs to the people, with its main strength lying

Arthur Freed, *Untitled, 1983*

Arthur Freed, *Untitled, 1983*

Arthur Freed, *Untitled, 1983*

in the folk-art tradition, not in an elitist niche." It was lovely to see a group of Minor's peers, artists and poets, yelling at each other and thoroughly enjoying their freedom to disagree.

At the end of that session we traveled down the coast to Carmel to visit Edward Weston, who was extremely ill at that time. His walk was a stooped shuffle. The main room was spare, and on a table were an avocado and a bowl of vegetables, which soon became the source of a joke: we were going to eat the subject matter for lunch. Later, Minor viewed some of Weston's prints, a few platinums and late things from Point Lobos, which was visible through a window of the house. The pictures were placed on the easel one at a time, the way they had always been, and the two men stood in silence, looking, for what was to be the last time, at those results of earlier opportunities. I believe that Weston showed us the way in. Through his attention to facts, both of photography and of place, unseen, felt knowledge was explicitly and intuitively located. Standing there, it seemed that they were performing some ancient ceremony. Weston had the appearance of an archivist, humble and proud of the things in his care. He offered them not as a reflection of his ego but as one still in need of examining them and sharing with others what could be learned in the process.

One sees in Minor's extensions of Weston's work at Point Lobos that beauty is the revolutionary work in art. Two artists, in the same place, created original forms to house their separate natures.

Perhaps no other photography teacher has so rigorously de-fined the study of art as a route to religion as Minor White. His process orientation was rare; ritual and the model of the master-teacher were met with suspicion. The controversy included accusations of "mind control" and "tampering." Other instructors encouraged us to view photographs as illustrations, nouns needing the qualification of text. Pictures considered successful confirmed rather than questioned. Any ambiguity was evidence of indecision, and mystery, as an aesthetic analogue of experience, was unacceptable.

The issue of autonomy is one that all good teachers face. The balance between independence and dependency plagues all of our consciences. One acknowledges the need to subordinate the ego in order to develop discipline, but one energetically defends the anarchy of the artist. Art is not therapy, but it has an unquestionable therapeutic effect. Spiritual values and self-image both contribute to a comprehensive understanding of creativity. The only criterion that seems practical is that the system should increase the ability to do original work.

It is disturbing to be confronted by the assumptions of childhood that severely limit the range of associations pictures can have. An instructor like Minor White helped us to change that habit. He demonstrated that art parallels experience, investing representation with clues to the secrets buried in ordinary life. This archaeology of the soul solicits statements some would prefer remained silent, but whose escape and transformation account for much of what we call quality and risk in art.

ARTHUR FREED

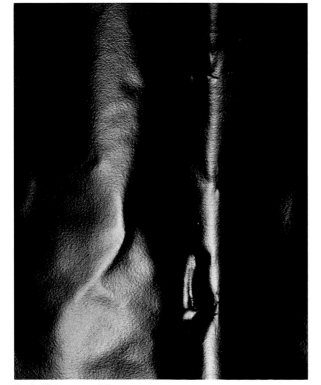

Carl Chiarenza, *Metonymy 255, 1982*

MY EXPOSURE TO MINOR WHITE coincided fortuitously with my exposure to Ralph Hattersley, Charles Arnold, Beaumont Newhall, Robert Koch (who taught literature and creative writing at Rochester Institute of Technology), and Frank Clement (who taught art appreciation). It was an unusual mix of creative visual minds, all involved in developing a new educational program focused on the artistic potential of photography. This was between 1955 and 1957, a time when Minor was also at an early stage of his own explorations through teaching, writing, editing, and picture making. As students we were in a very real sense guinea pigs. For some of us the mixture of tastes was too rich to handle; for others it sparked unforeseen possibilities that we would realize only when we had left Rochester and encountered other ideas.

It is impossible to isolate exactly what Minor did for me. But two things seem clear: he provided support for a belief in the photograph as an object worthy of intense effort in the making, and in the photograph as an object in and of itself, apart from anything else in the world, that could be as expressive as music, poetry, or painting in relating the individual to the world.

CARL CHIARENZA

A Tribute to Minor White

ROGER LIPSEY

Minor White, *Bristol, Vermont, 1971*

THE MAIN IMPORTANCE of Minor lies not in that he was a friend of this or that individual's, nor that he studied one or another esoteric philosophy, nor even that he wrote of such things, but in that he made some classically great photographs. He rendered a service to later generations of photographers by enlarging on the mystique of seeing that Stieglitz first expressed, but Minor's writings on the subject seem blurred in a way that his photographs are not: a little amateurish, a little enthusiastic, too sure of the abstract, oddly personal and idiosyncratic although based in a general way on various cohesive bodies of thought and practice. All of these writings are a finger pointing at the sun, and whether it is off by a degree or two from dead center hardly matters, since younger photographers and artists will not fail to get a general sense of direction.

The best of his photographs have something of the profundity and simple directness that he admired in the writings of the great religious teachers. In the exhibition and accompanying catalogue *Octave of Prayer* presented at Massachusetts Institute of Technology in 1972, Minor included only one of his own photographs in this extensive selection. It is at first glance a drier photograph than one usually associates with his work, more like the later landscapes of Edward Weston than Minor's lyrical art. As a document, it shows what appears to be a road with a spotty pattern of snow and marked by the passage of

tires. In the upper third of the image stands a pyramidal boulder—a double pyramid, in fact—dusted with bright snow, hedged around by a few trees and bushes, and standing out crisply against the dark and indistinct woods behind it. In the context of this exhibition, and particularly in light of the book's extensive introduction on the degrees of prayer and the photographic image as a visible equivalent of the invisible, we should take appreciation of this winter landscape beyond acknowledging its physical elements and perhaps admiring its formal structure (something indeed could be said about its harmony of rectilinear and oblique lines, and the cognate outlines of the bare roadway to the left and the boulder above). I am looking for Minor's intention in this image, yet the subtler intentions of an artist are often best left in the shell, like a sea creature that perishes when it is torn from its housing. The dilemma suggested by this simile is dispelled by the thought that intentions are common property, expressed in one way by the photographer and in another by a viewer, exhausted by neither. It will only perish, or seem dreary and pointless, if the viewer fails to house it with the kind of care that the photographer exercised.

The photograph is a classic image of two worlds: below, the horizontal world of time, change, and motion, appearance and disappearance; above, the world of permanence, of light shining from the darkness, of vertical ascent and the holy mountain. Below, a world trafficked in both senses by man; above, a pristine world that invites him. While stating this immemorially old proposition, the photograph remains a landscape vignette of the American Northeast and so is an image of two worlds in this sense also. The physical presence and familiarity of this landscape protect the viewer from an excess of abstraction, from thoughts that start solid with the memory of the two worlds and quickly dissipate into footnotes. Every element of the photograph functions sensuously and, as medieval thinkers put it, supersensually: for example, the trees and bushes that partially obscure the boulder add variety as line and texture but also communicate a sense of the mountain's distance and relative inaccessibility—a thought that Minor expressed in other terms in his introductory discussion of prayer.

I can remember showing Minor's work to a class in the history of photography. It was the first time that I had done so, and I had no idea what to expect. The slides passed by one after another as I summarized Minor's career and established his point of view on camerawork, until gradually I grew more silent in response to a silence that had settled on the class. We continued the survey of Minor's work with hardly a comment, apart from a few titles and dates, and broke class early since everyone seemed to think it appropriate. What was in the air, then? Some kind of Q.E.D., I thought: it had been demonstrated that Minor White, for all his human weaknesses and confusions (no doubt far fewer than in the majority of men and women) had attained to a degree of art, somewhere in the Octave, that could move, delight, and teach—an art that makes a difference.

The Spring-tight Line

ROBERT ADAMS

MINOR WHITE BELIEVED that photography was a way to know, and might even have agreed with Henry Miller, who said once that art will die away when we all learn enough. White's fundamental conviction that good pictures have to match up accurately with life is, I think, incontrovertible. One need only cite as evidence the fact that nobody can talk us into liking a picture. That just happens, suddenly one morning or slowly over a season, when a picture or the recollection of it aligns with our experience.

That in any case is how I came to value certain of White's landscapes. I lived on the Oregon coast near a spectacular, often fog-shrouded headland; on clear days one could see from its summit across fields of salal, down hundreds of feet of rock, and finally out over the ocean. It was like parts of the Bay Area coast, and I began to understand, far from museums and art magazines, just how reverently White had paid attention to what he saw in California.

It was White's gift, I think, to understand passionately the limits of documentary photography narrowly defined. "The objectivity of the camera, used wrongly," he observed, "is the very devil." He knew that great pictures cannot be just about particular landscapes; they have to direct us to more, even eventually to the whole of life. If they do not, then "the documentary photograph, the literal image, is the ultimate illusion."

White's choice of the ocean as a subject was, I think, for him exactly right. Its appearance, closely observed, is hypnotic; who can be uninterested in so delicate a light, or the power of waves on rock, or the immensity of the whole view? White's pictures come to more, however, than just these geographic facts, as anyone who has walked the beach almost knows they must. The ocean, by virtue of its size and apparent emptiness, invites attention outward from our petty landscapes, away from ourselves. (White said once that he was "appalled by the image of [his] inner landscape.") The sea is too vast to understand and too awesome to avoid; it attracts us as it offers a final liberation from human scale. All this coincided richly with White's understanding of art as metaphor, as a suggestion of similarities between the known and the barely known.

If it was White's achievement to show us that photographs can point beyond themselves, it was his fate as a human being, limited like the rest of us, sometimes to fail. But because his goals were major, the failures are not entirely failures: they have value as they are instructive. And White, who was a fully committed teacher, would I think have told us to use whichever of his pictures help.

One can begin by noting that White himself sensed a potential problem in what he wanted to do. He observed hopefully, referring to some of his own work, that "the spring-tight line

Minor White, *Surf Vertical, San Mateo County,* from *Song Without Words, 1947*

between reality and photograph has been stretched relentlessly, but it has not been broken. These abstractions of nature have not left the world of appearances; for to do so is to break the camera's strongest point—its authenticity." At his best, White made pictures that were strong with that authenticity, the appearance of the world. When he failed it was because, I think, he tried to escape it, to travel to what e. e. cummings once sardonically called the "hell of a good universe next door." Because we all have wanted to make that trip, in sheer weariness with home, we can sympathize, but because there is no hope of reaching such a destination short of death we are obliged, I think, to resist it.

The problem of an art in flight from "the world of appearances" was not uniquely White's. I would trade all of Stieglitz's pictures of blurry night clouds for a single hard view of the sky in daylight, and especially one of those where he nicked in a little solidifying foliage from the ground where we walk. The same issue, in slightly different form, has always plagued fiction: writers struggle with the temptation to write allegory, airy stuff where characters walk stiffly around wearing signs instead of slouching ambiguously past like our neighbors and only afterward coming to represent more than just themselves. William

Carlos Williams synopsized, in famous lines, the practice that seems most durable: "through metaphor to reconcile/ the people and the stones./ Compose. (No ideas/ but in things)." Ideas can only be in things if the things are credible as specifics. And that requires, I think, in the case of pictures, that there be an indication of the subject's actual size.

White turned away from literal geography when he made landscapes that omit an indication of scale. The pictures range from what I presume might be medium shots to close-ups, but the practice in all of them is so thoroughly to deny a viewer clues to size that the difference does not matter. We cannot grasp with certainty whether the literal geography is composed of sand or gravel, whether a view is an examination of disintegrating plaster or an aerial.

Why did White do this? I sense, when the practice is considered together with the narrow range of his subject matter, a struggle with the world of appearances that must have at times been extreme, and from which escape must have been attractive—though I can also appreciate that the formulation of landscapes without scale might have seemed to him an appropriate pedagogical tactic, however ironically counterproductive it seems to me, for leading students to look at life. If the whole of

Minor White, *Bullet Holes, Capitol Reef, Utah, 1961*, from *Sequence 17*

Minor White, *Dry Stream Bed, Wotem, Utah,* from *Sequence 1967*

Creation can be found in its smallest fragment, why not try to suggest this by withholding indications of scale? And so we find not only pictures in which this is done but others where he sets out positively to upset our preconceptions about size, as in some of the views made in Utah where he radically combines what is close and far.

The erasure of identifiable scale is augmented, of course, by other practices that discourage viewers from knowing what the pictures are literally of. Even in the sequence of coastal pictures, "Song Without Words," he chose to upend one of the seascapes so that we are compelled to see it first as pure shape. And his relegation of captions to the end of *Mirrors, Messages, Manifestations,* a large book, effectively forces us to encounter many of the pictures as abstractions. (One of the captions—"Bullet Holes, Capitol Reef, Utah"—transforms a rich but puzzling photograph into a great one. With the caption we see at once two subjects: the damage by gunfire, and a constellation of stars; in what other picture is our digust arrested so sharply by wonder?)

White did make beautiful landscapes that are *nearly* unidentifiable. They are, though, never wholly cut away from the recognizable world. I think particularly of the calligraphic reflection in water above the dam, and of the bird-shaped shadow on the white canyon wall. In these pictures the setting requires a moment's study to identify, but it can be done. And once it is done, we can look again at the calligraphy or bird and feel

the astonishment that White intended us to feel: how extraordinary the commonplace world can be—miracles can come from it. But again, the context is essential: miracles alone, without the norm, are not really miracles at all. Without the setting of the identifiable world we are unconvinced of White's transcendental truths because we are not allowed to experience the conditions of their discovery.

It should be said that the question of how close a photograph ought to stick to the outward appearance of life, even when describing miracles, is not necessarily best answered by the literal minded. Aristotle argued that it was legitimate for playwrights to include "probable improbabilities," things that were unbelievable except within a playwright's imaginary world on stage, provided that the overall production revealed truths about life as we experience it off stage. The general success of White's infrared landscapes can be understood, I think, on these grounds.

My favorite of White's infrared pictures is the one of the poplars along the road near Dansville, New York. In the brilliant leaves there is a discovery: many trees, though they are in fact usually dark, *seem* to be full of light, perhaps because the leaves, especially poplar leaves and especially in the wind, reflect it. In any case, when I look at the picture I think of Williams's beautiful line "there is a bird in the poplars—it is the sun!" White's metaphor is simpler—there is *light* in the poplars, it is the sun—but it is a likeness that is, in its visual expression, just as lovely.

I have said that certain of White's landscapes seem to me

Minor White, *Road and Poplar Trees,* from *Sequence 10, 1955*

There is a bird in the poplars—it is the sun! WILLIAM CARLOS WILLIAMS

unsuccessful because they fail to convey a clear indication of scale and are thus not identifiably of the world we know. It can be argued that in this I am simply rejecting the romantic vision, and that it is unprofitable to dispute matters of belief. Which is probably true. But it seems necessary to try to argue the point because the abstractions come to a closed landscape where, lost in our private dreams, we can no longer communicate. Sooner or later one has to ask of all pictures what kind of life they promote (or, as White phrased it, "Do your photographs offer . . . sustenance?"), and some of these views suggest to me a frightening alienation from "the world of appearances."

The beauty of the seascapes offers an alternative. White's goal with them was presumably the same—to convey a sense of the mysterious, limitless nature of the Creation—but they, unlike the abstractions, also convey peace. It is a calm defined through metaphor: oceanic scale is the scale of eternity. Such a testament is itself baffling, but we are encouraged to try to understand it by its provision of a place to begin. We can, as White did, walk the shore.

"The Spring-tight Line" was originally written for this issue of *Aperture* and appears in an edited form in *Beauty in Photography: Essays in Defense of Traditional Values.*

MINOR DISCUSSED world problems infrequently. I did talk with him about how I thought the life at the house in Arlington was extraordinary because it seemed almost grotesquely sheltered. It seemed so clean, white walled, and peaceful, like a promise of a better world. Conversely, I thought it was terribly escapist in the context of the times. I asked him, "How can you justify what appears to be such an escapist life?" As I remember, he said he had devoted his life to peaceful pursuit, to another way, and his life, too, was full of conflicts.

I went straight out and became a news photographer. I didn't have a feeling of a split between Minor's photography and what I wanted to do. When I was in class and saw Minor's work, I was very comfortable with it. I don't know if I totally understood where it came from, but I understood what it meant to me. I enjoyed it. Once you have studied with a person like Minor and have looked closely at photographs that you consider significant, you can't go back to being a slob. I left Minor and went on to become a serious photographer. What Minor gave me was the sense that I was about to put my soul and ideas out there and there were no excuses. He was merciless in his examination of your work, and it was exactly what I needed to send me out.

I never knew if Minor was a wise man, because he would come out with one-liners that were sometimes very abrasive but had a truth about them. Then he wouldn't go any further. It was one of his best and worst characteristics. On one of our last social occasions together, I went to dinner at Minor's house. There were a lot of people there, and he began discussing my photography. Sitting across the table he made a pronouncement: "Gene photographs people being eaten." At the time I was hurt; I thought it a little vicious. Then I got away from it, though it stuck in my head, and I realized there was probably truth in it. To have made the statement without going any further, however, didn't seem very helpful. He wasn't making a value judgment: he was saying, "This is what you do. You're not going to change."

Eugene Richards, *West Memphis, Arkansas, 1971*

Minor taught by experience and ideas rather than by exterior materials and information. He talked about a total creative process. This meant you had to live the life of what you were going to become rather than simply adopt a certain style of photography.

EUGENE RICHARDS

Eugene Richards, *Funeral at Doe Lake, West Memphis, Arkansas, 1971*

Edward Ranney, *Near Temple Sowerty, Cumbria, England, 1980*

It is important to both study history and work within nature. Art brings together the work of nature and the work of man. The work of art does not stand by itself; it is a chunk of nature highly encrusted by man. To study art we need to study nature. The more alive we are, the more we tend to go back to what is written about the world and to the world itself; between these we reinforce our desires.

FREDERICK SOMMER, from "From the Birth of Art to Aesthetics," 1982

WITH ATTENTION to the now more fully published legacies of photographers such as Timothy O'Sullivan, Carleton Watkins, Eugène Atget, and Alfred Stieglitz, it has become ever more clear to me that those bodies of photographic work that have gained in meaning are those that originally found their vision in the external world. In doing so they have created their own inner world, while leaving us free to return to the external world with renewed respect and energy. How this might occur today varies, of course, with the personality and intent of each worker, as well as his point of entry both to his time and the history of the medium.

In the dislocated times of the mid- to late sixties, it was the

Edward Ranney, *Rio Grande Gorge, New Mexico, 1978*

vision and work of Edward Weston that sustained me in my early efforts in photography. At a time in our culture when it was imperative for sensibility to withhold consent from war and society, I was determined to work independently in photography, at a distance from living heroes in the medium. It was not until 1970, when some work had proved itself through time, that it became important to meet and share with Paul Caponigro an energy and awareness gained from photographing certain ancient sites and stones.

My own entry to the metaphysical landscape of ancient culture had initially been as a student living within the world of the Quechua Indians, near Cuzco, Peru. The concerns of my photographic work, while solitary, were often shared and encouraged by colleagues of Indian descent, as well as by artists, historians, and scientists. My commitment to photograph the remains of Inca stonework throughout the seventies was intimately related both to my feeling for the subject and to a need to establish a context of collective cultural meaning within which my work would have its place. *Monuments of the Incas* therefore became a multidisciplinary undertaking, one not strictly photographic in all its concerns, but nevertheless a work still deeply concerned with a photographic view of the world. In spite of the compromises and costs involved, the book form remains the most relevant and enduring context for photog-

Edward Ranney, *Saltworks, near Urabamba, Peru, 1975*

raphy in our culture. If it is an expression of vision and not self-promotion, the book is, in fact, the key format today in which a photographic statement can come closest to the integral role art once played in ancient culture.

The republication in 1969 of Robert Frank's The *Americans*, the same year that saw Minor White's *Mirrors, Messages, Manifestations* in print, was to me a significant moment for photography in American culture. Beyond its political and social concerns, Frank's book implicitly asked what relevance a more formal language such as traditional landscape photography could have. By 1975, the year before Minor White's death, the nominally "styleless" landscape documents known as "New Top-

ographics" had brought attention to the inherently complex nature of photographic style and meaning, as well as to the continually narrowing sense of time and space of the contemporary American landscape. Embattled sensibility, wishing perhaps not to take refuge in art but rather to find an appropriate expression of life, however minimal, asked us to turn away from diminished icons, from form without meaning.

We are at a point in culture, as Lucy Lippard has written in *Overlay*, in which ". . . if art is for some people a substitute for religion, it is a pathetically inadequate one because of its rupture from social life and from the heterogeneous value systems that exist below the surface of a homogenized dominant

Stone upon stone, and man, where was he? PABLO NERUDA, from *Heights of Machu Picchu*

Edward Ranney, *Crook Holme Hill, Cumbria, England, 1980*

culture." Lippard also suggests, in discussing the implications of developments in environmental and performance art, that we are now seeing a reassertion of the social function of art that, as in primal or ancient cultures, affects people in a way substantially different from art that is "simply one more manipulable commodity in a market society where even ideas and the deepest expressions of human emotion are absorbed and controlled." Minor White's problematic legacy may have more to teach us now, as much for the inherent limitations of teaching only a self-referential kind of art, as for its searching quality, than it did during the last decades of his life.

EDWARD RANNEY

To the photographer temperamentally compelled to work inwardly his medium forces him to use the outward landscape to manifest by way of metaphor the inner reality. He has little more choice in this than the temperamentally compelled outward-going photographer has in his choice of tradition. Consequently the tradition of the Equivalent came into photography, if not Stieglitz first then someone else would have, and the contemporary Caponigros will sustain the tradition because by nature they can not do otherwise.

MINOR WHITE, *Aperture,* 1964

I MET MINOR WHITE in 1953 through Benjamin Chin, with whom I studied photography in San Francisco during my tour of duty with the U.S. Army. Benny had been a student of Ansel Adams's and Minor White's in the late forties at the California School of Fine Arts and had encouraged me to study with Minor. Benny thought my way of seeing was closely related to the West Coast tradition of photography, which was concerned with superb craft and form. He suggested I work with someone like Minor to develop another way of thinking about photography.

The evening I met Minor was the occasion of a farewell party for him given at Ansel Adams's studio. He was leaving for a position at George Eastman House in Rochester, New York.

In the three years between that introduction and my first encounter with him as a student, I was discharged from the Army, spent some time in Boston, and returned to San Francisco, where I was exposed to individuals who were involved with photographing the grand natural landscape in all its power, as well as to people who were familiar with Minor's ideas. After almost a year in California I grew dissatisfied with my pursuits—something was missing, though I couldn't grasp exactly what it was. And then something happened: a retrospective of the paintings of Morris Graves at the San Francisco Museum of Modern Art opened my eyes. I was so struck by this work that I immediately realized what had been lacking in my work with the camera:

Paul Caponigro, *San Sebastian, New Mexico, 1980*

To photograph not for what the subject is, but for what else it is.

that mystical quality, depth of insight, and penetration of nature manifest in Graves's work is what I desired to see in my photography. My subconscious leaped at the recognition, and within two weeks I packed my bags and left for the East Coast.

From all I heard and what little I saw of Minor White's work, it seemed that he came closest to what I felt about Morris Graves. Resolved to study with White one day, I wrote asking for a meeting and enclosed a portfolio of my work. In the fall of 1957 he invited me to come and live as an apprentice along with a few other students. I stayed on into December, helping with subscriptions to *Aperture*, which Minor was editing at the time, and assisting him in the darkroom. We all made field trips, separately and together, but most of the activity around the house at 72 North Union Street centered on looking at work and "reading" photographs, an activity that involved sitting in front of a photograph long enough for something to happen, to possibly break through to "what else the photograph is."

The atmosphere at Minor's place was quite beautiful. A spirit of cooperation mingled with good music, creating an almost dizzying kind of "special perfume" that we all inhaled. I felt that Minor carried the beauty of craft from the West and placed it on his walls in Rochester. In the sparsity and simplicity of the house a sense of Zen was achieved. We were encouraged to read Eugen Herrigel's *Zen in the Art of Archery* and Boles-lavsky's *Acting: The First Six Lessons*. We were encouraged to meditate. Minor was reading P. D. Ouspensky's *In Search of the Miraculous* at the time. All of this was certainly interesting, but I was far more intrigued with Minor's work, both the photographs he was then making and work he'd done in the period prior to his move east.

I was taken by the fact that he could put on a piece of photographic paper a certain kind of imagery that did what he sought to do: to photograph for what else the subject is. In a way, he laid himself bare through his images. There was a good lesson to be had in his use of the "Sequence," which he called "a cinema of stills." By arranging a dozen or more photographs in a specific sequence (obviously a meaning was intended), he aimed at borrowing elements from each of the photographs and lending each of the images in the sequence new ideas and possible interpretations. A kind of story telling emerged. The sequences could be read in as many ways as there were students to look at them, but on occasion Minor would indicate that a few students had understood, in spirit or feeling, the theme he had intended.

Minor was indicating a way to approach the seeing of images. A kernel of the teaching was to break away from the associative, a very good device for opening one to other possibilities, but the device could also lead to oversymbolizing. This also carried over into the actual photographing: either Minor expected the student to arrive somewhere specific in the "reading" of images, or possibly he was experimenting to see where it all might lead. A lot of experimenting was in process. He would put you in a room alone with a few photographs and give you the task of relating your experience to the images. Sustained concentration was not always that easy, though; meaning did not always congeal from the complexity of the stuff in that photographic space mounted on a board or pinned to a wall. An insistence on finding meaning could hinder the possibility of simple seeing and intuitive understanding.

I traveled cross country with Minor in 1959, camping and photographing with him and assisting with his workshops in Portland, Oregon, and in San Francisco. The students loved and revered him, but a major complaint persisted among the more skeptical: why did they have to see things, and especially faces, in the photographs put up for the purpose of "reading"? It annoyed some, intrigued others. But most of his students loved him for his generosity, energy, and caring. He had the respect of many simply because his dedication to the medium always shone forth; he worked seemingly without end.

We often heard about Stieglitz and the concept of the Equivalent from Minor. In all the time I was with Minor I never really understood what he was saying about Equivalence. Most of his students were trying desperately to make an equivalent, an achievement that marked the graduation from mere photographing to "real" photography. It seemed the idea of equivalence reflected the simple recognition of the unity of all things, the recognition of great principles operating in many things on many levels. Artists and poets of all mediums and from all times have had this awareness of linking principles and have attempted to make this awareness a primary tool for creation. Zen masters of painting seldom act until personal motivation is supplanted by the greater forces and combine with their being to create an act that includes the whole. They strive to become a part of a greater action. Self-expression is not enough for the Zen master. Imitation without understanding serves only to delay contact with the universals.

Minor was attracted to this idea of Zen and, I feel, took hold of it intellectually as most of us are prone to do. Making the transition to the actuality, however, requires a great leap. Without the depth of one's total being, the great ideas we talked about could only be sensed. I believe that Minor strove to make equivalents as he understood equivalence, from the inspiration of Stieglitz. Stieglitz saw power in those things that he chose to photograph, and frequently managed to demonstrate that power in the image or, at least, provided a suggestion of that power. *Recognition* of the flow of power was the link between Stieglitz and his subjects. I feel that Minor interrupted the flow with too much personal concern. Consequently, Minor's energy was dispersed into the ideas about equivalence and too often worked toward a formula that he hoped would eventually get him to the desired place. His early work was intuitive and full of aspiration; certainly, Minor's images are very poetic and beautiful and often psychologically potent, but an inner thrashing and laboring is also evident. Minor did well in catching reflections of himself in his images, but I never felt that they carried that extra measure of power so evident in the work of Stieglitz.

We were all enamored of the atmosphere created by the person, and it was without question one of beauty and honest work, but I seldom felt that the overall situation allowed for clarity. There were too many delicious garden paths down which to be led. Too many attractive ideas. The multitude of methods put forth—Gurdjieff dances, "six lessons in acting," hypnosis, Zen teachings—suggested that Minor was basically insecure about his stance in photography or, perhaps, in his life. The point may have been to try and increase one's awareness through exercises, a most desirable state not so easily attained. Minor sought to make photography *conscious*, as he understood the Gurdjieffian meaning of the word. He was writing a manual on the matter while in Arlington, Massachusetts. Always the latest work on the spiritual quest, such as the escapades of Carlos Castaneda and Don Juan, would be taken up by Minor and incorporated into his teaching of photography. One method fully understood should have served. Many methods reshaped and partially understood was vague and nebulous, not unlike attending a séance. It left things cosmically cloudy. In his well-meaning attempts to raise the level of photography (and photographs), Minor overembellished the process and failed to put photography in its right place.

I recall once meeting Paul Strand, who of course had known Stieglitz. I asked Strand what he understood by the idea of the Equivalent. He related to me a story of visiting Stieglitz: as soon as he got off the elevator of the building of "291" and before he rounded the corner to the gallery, Stieglitz would begin talking at him. I gathered from this story that Stieglitz was fond of holding forth. Regarding the Equivalent, Strand said, "I always have felt that photographing was a much simpler act than that." I understood Strand to mean that a simple state of knowing and doing too often became confused or interrupted by a complicated idea.

My conclusion was that the simplicity and directness of the act could put one in touch with a process that might result in an Equivalent. I see it as holding a state of pure and deep recognition. You must be aware of a good state and use it, rather than think that an exercise before clicking the shutter is going to do something for you. Minor's early photographs, I feel, were charged with love of work and with aspiration. He

sensed something marvelous with which he desired greater contact.

In the years that I knew him, Minor attempted to formulate a method and teach creativity. In my opinion, this method was not in accordance with the essentials of the creative process. If one has engaged photography fully and with understanding and direction, it is enough in itself and offers depth of experience. Correct orientation to the self and one's materials holds the key to a greater action. In my experience and in communicating with others about their experience, silence is one of the great traditions of teaching spirit. Apprentices are asked to sweep, observe, serve, and be silent in order to eventually acquire the greater action. Time and specifics do not burden or condition the atmosphere of such a situation.

There was something admirable and infectious about Minor's exuberance and sense of adventure, something of a childlike aspiration. He was also a kitten at times, bouncing off walls and leaping in the air only to be surprised at where he had landed. There was also something quixotic in his activities, noble in purpose, but misdirected.

Obviously I have brought to the surface some long-standing questions, not about Minor but about the meaning of engaging in a craft for more than producing objects. I am grateful to Minor for so generously providing the abundance of positive elements and the sheer love and energy of working with photography. I am equally grateful to Minor for providing me with contradictions and contrasts regarding an approach to the way of the spirit. Minor was one of the most human of individuals, possessed of the failings, sufferings, and potentials we all carry. In certain areas he stood out like a Santa Claus for photographers, one of his greatest gifts being *Aperture* magazine, which helped the established and the young photographers to pursue camerawork as a fine art. It gave warmth to that cool world of anonymity and unacceptance experienced by the few pioneers of the medium. His loving care was exhibited by his insistence that the images of these fine artists be treated with respect and that the inherent beauty of their craft be evident through fine reproduction. The periodical was a pace setter and traveled a long distance from the very ordinary reproductions offered by other publications. With *Aperture*, Minor again demonstrated tireless effort and devotion.

PAUL CAPONIGRO

But if painting and sculpture do not communicate they induce an attitude of communion and contemplation. They offer to many an equivalent of what is regarded as part of religious life: a sincere and humble submission to a spiritual object, an experience which is not given automatically, but requires preparation and purity of spirit.

MEYER SCHAPIRO

Robert Bourdeau, *Sri Lanka, 1978*

I FIRST MET MINOR in 1959, and for about five years we engaged in informal talks concerning photography and vision. What he gave me was a way of looking at things rather than a way of working—an incentive to put down in pictorial form that thing that I loved. The principles of Minor's philosophy, which combined the meditative approach with a high degree of disciplined craftsmanship, struck a responsive chord in me. Through him I gained a love and respect for camerawork, for the landscape, and for photography's way of seeing. However, I knew from the start I had to find my own vision.

I have striven for a fuller, more realized image, a sense of mystery, a presence, and a kind of spirituality. I want my images to be tapestries, where the entire surface of the print has a life force full of revelation, lucidity, activity, and plenitude—a visual/emotional completeness.

ROBERT BOURDEAU

Robert Bourdeau, *Ontario, 1981*

Upon confronting a difficult or puzzling photograph, an individual must decide whether the artist is being unecessarily obscure or the viewer, himself, is being unduly obtuse. We should be cautious about resolving all such questions in our favor . . .

HENRY HOLMES SMITH

Robert Bourdeau, *Ontario, 1979*

William Giles, *Bubbles, Sea Ranch, California, 1973*

octave for minor

stroke by stroke
the calligrapher
scribed the void

from that stylus
quietness flowed
a thousand miles

this tabula rasa
mind was printed
with his letters

his words became
the constituents
of our intellect

as his testament
has been written
in a pupil's eye

so it is written
His finger wrote
upon this ground

inside this four
dimensioned mind
his stylus moves

beyond his death
his stela stands
on living stones

WILLIAM SMITH

John Yang, *Audubon Center, Greenwich, Connecticut, 1979*

John Yang, *Millbrook Mountain, Mohonk Preserve on the
Shawangunk Ridge, Ulster County, N.Y., 1980*

Though leaves are many, the root is one;
Through all the lying days of my youth
I swayed my leaves and flowers in the sun;
Now I may wither into the truth.

W. B. YEATS, "The Coming of Wisdom with Time"

John Yang, *Long Pond Preserve of the Nature Conservancy,*
Waccabuc, Westchester County, N.Y., 1979

Only a small crash in the kitchen, but enough to shatter my calm and a bowl. One careless glance caught the pieces—white porcelain still quivering on the floor—a rice bowl, pleasant in subtle curve, from Japan, delicate to balance, was no more. He who dropped it fingered the pieces. He was silent and, I suppose, sad. I turned back to preceding thoughts. Then he was jubilant. One fragment, he exclaimed, "has a form." And truly he pointed to one that was haunting to see....

And since I make photographs it seemed natural to transmute yet again and make a photograph of it; to train my camera on the splinter seemed obviously the next step. But a thought stopped me. What is the status of a photograph of an object that has just found its own form? A copy? Or a photograph that in turn would find a form peculiar to itself?

There wasn't time to think through such questions in the chain reaction of thoughts that followed the explosion. In the "fallout," however, I found a name for some of my own photographs. I always photograph found objects; excepting portraits, all of my photographs are of found objects. And now, thinking of the best of them, I hear little crashes tinkling back twenty years, for the best of them have always been photographs that found themselves....

MINOR WHITE, "Found Photographs," from "Memorable Fancies," 1957

Frederick Sommer, *Glass, 1943*

Once, Minor called and woke me up at dawn to say that he had just got out of hospital after a heart attack. It so upset me I threw the I Ching *for him, as we had done many times for each other. The hexagram that came up was* The Wanderer. *When you delve into that form of mentality you get more than an image. It is a highly sophisticated way of using your mind, which ancient people knew about. There is no chance involved at all. It is like the mystique of the Found Object. There was no chance because who found it anyway? Someone RE-COGNIZED it.*
WALTER CHAPPELL

氣　ch'i:　vapor, breath, air, manner, influence, weather
　　　Ch'i:　Breath of Heaven, Spirit, Vital Force

The vision of *The I Ching or Book of Changes* was a discipline that Minor White actively embraced. A project he conceived but never completed was to photograph images equivalent to the sixty-four hexagrams of the book. Robert Mahon has applied the book to an existing negative. A multiple portrait surfaces. Its revelations are fragments that encourage us to rearrange our sense of the complete image. It becomes a metaphor close to the diverse legacy of Minor himself and the multiple faces of his own identity.

FROM JOHN CAGE I learned about the ancient Chinese oracle, *The I Ching or Book of Changes*, and how it is related to chance. Using the book's sixty-four hexagrams, I applied the principle of chance operations to steps in the photographic process by considering the components that contribute to a photograph: angle of view, composition, and various aesthetic factors on the one hand, and shutter speed, development time, and different technical matters on the other. The two-hundred-and-sixteen-image portrait of John Cage that resulted was very different from any portrait I might have made according to a preconceived aesthetic view. The process taught me that chance in conjunction with photography is a way to free my visual perception from habit. The work is experimental; it becomes a way to discover something I had never seen before. I committed myself to this way of working so that personal biases or prejudices would not limit the possibilities and I would be allowed unimagined images, photographs made remarkable precisely because they had not been previously envisioned.

In 1982 I made a group of photographs from inherited negatives. Using these procedures I made something new from old materials. *Bathers* is such an example. The subject is a familiar one: a young couple sitting on a beach. The subtle details in this image interested me: the sexuality of the woman; her obvious infatuation with the man; his probable indifference; the language of their hands, legs, and eyes; as well as the many vaguely recognizable objects and figures in the background. The negative was telling a story about a person in my family, and I wanted to examine it more closely.

The original image is never seen in its entirety since each new photograph is a fragment of the whole. The eye scans the fragments and the mind attempts to reconstruct the scene. A depth of understanding that would be unattainable in a single view derives from the highlighting, obscuring, and concentration on different parts. A complexity of characters, place, and narrative is revealed that might have been overlooked in a simple snapshot.

I seek to understand the moment that has been captured by the camera. I explore the potential of the negative and observe its limitless variety. This process is comparable to a law of the physical world: a finite line can be divided into an infinite number of segments. Knowledge of the line increases with the quantity of measured parts, but the knowledge can never be complete or absolute. The possibilities are endless.

ROBERT MAHON

Robert Mahon, *Bathers, 1982*

Abe Frajndlich, *Form and Face, Boston, Mass.,*
May 14, 1976

Abe Frajndlich, *Mirror, 203 Park Avenue, May 16, 1976*

Abe Frajndlich, *Minor White, Boston, Mass., May 14, 1976*

Abe Frajndlich, *Composite Portrait, 203 Park Avenue,*
May 4, 1976

I WAS TWENTY-FOUR when I attended [Minor's] Cleveland workshop. . . . I had just begun to take photographs. . . . I . . . arrived at the first day's workshop twenty minutes late. A slide was on the screen. About fifty people were on the floor. The room was dark and filled with Minor's low, almost chanting, voice.

The more I listened, the more intrigued I became. . . . [The] teacher in him . . . captured my imagination. He opened up the multiple levels of a color slide of two footprints in wet sand by telling us: "In the life of every man, there comes a point when he walks on water."

Minor used ritual to keep himself and his students alert to life's possibilities. His insistence on ritual stemmed from his commitment to Gurdjieff's philosophy. Part of his philosophy, too, was his conviction that photography was not a parlor game or a weekend activity, but . . . was as essential to our lives as breathing.

Minor constantly put us through exercises to enlarge our sensitivity to photographs. He was interested in the reactions a print could engender in the viewer. We were urged to tune our bodies to the making of an image, to suspend the whole rational process. Minor also had a knack for leading us into deeper waters. "Just get into the confusion," he would say. "Just be confused. Quit trying to be clear. Quit putting such a premium on clarity."

ABE FRAJNDLICH, from *Lives I've Never Lived:*
A Portrait of Minor White

I LIVED AT MINOR'S house in Arlington in 1971 and 1972. I saw Minor play and live his roles as a photographer, photography teacher, department chairman, workshop leader, student/teacher of Gurdjieff, counselor, and friend. Our bond of friendship grew.

During the months before his illness, while I was living with the woman who is now my wife, Minor would call on the phone and ask if we wouldn't mind his coming over for a visit. Of course we would scurry about cleaning things up, discussing how out of character it was for Minor to drop in.

Minor returned to the hospital for the last time after months of involvement with lawyers, legal problems, and doctors. Our main concern was to have Minor as free of tubes and drugs as possible, according to his wishes. Mrs. D., a very close friend of Minor's, and I were working closely with the doctors and nurses. One evening during dinner, I remember calling the hospital to check on the situation and was told that Minor had been repeating my name and asking that I be there with him. I immediately returned and began a twenty-hour experience that was a lifetime in itself. Minor would drift in and out of sleep and describe what he saw, and there in his darkened room, my hand in his, I began to see the same images. We were able to talk about them. At times when his fear or anxiety seemed to swell, I could help him return to the small wooden rowboat we were in as we drifted from one shore to another. Minor's description of an intense white light became visible for me. I knew I was hallucinating. It was the early hours of the morning, I was exhausted from weeks of emotional pressure, yet those hallucinations were clear. I was on this voyage. There were interruptions, nurses whispering, snapping me from the comfort of the boat. But always I would return.

When we finally arrived at the other shore, it was time to say good-bye. I felt I had to make a choice. I could step off the boat and enter this new realm or return. Minor was gone— although still hours away from his last breath. Did we say our good-bye in a hospital room or on that shore?

For many hours I sat with him after that good-bye. Minor's last words were "higher, higher." Did Minor mean, if we must put meaning to them, that his spirit was reaching new heights, or that we should elevate our goals, or that he was being lifted from this bodily plane to an ethereal one, or might he have been requesting to be propped up higher in his bed so as to make his breathing easier? I believe those words, and what already has been done with them, encapsulate the myth around Minor. It is the ambiguity that is the key.

Minor as a teacher created a situation that at times he controlled, and at times he didn't. The myth preceded him, and maybe his fault is that he did nothing to prevent it. He created an atmosphere for constantly questioning ideas or responses. It is we who must judge how we question the decision process in ourselves.

PETER LAYTIN

Jerry N. Uelsmann, *Untitled, 1982*

Creating the Space

DRID WILLIAMS

Minor White, *Drid Williams, Capitol Reef, Utah,*
from *Sequence 17, 1962*

MINOR CAME FROM MINNESOTA. That was significant because of the sense of space he grew up with. Minnesota has forests, lakes, the Iron Range, and a feeling—like all of the plains states—of unbounded space. It is flat. Hot like the bottom of a frying pan in summer and cold like an icebox in winter. There are wild extremes: punishing hardship and delicate subtleties. Unlike the Pacific Northwest, which is dominated by the vertical dimensions of mountains and evergreens, a winter landscape in Minnesota is sparse, Zenlike; endless reaches of different white hues and subtle tans, grays, blues delicately accented with black. It is also a place that someone like Minor would want to get away from. This shows in his work. He had a sense of living in a world that has no limits; that he could travel, and that he could meet people with whom he could communicate. The very expanse of his native state gave him a sense of fewer limitations.

I met Minor in 1957 through Bill Smith, whom I had known since I was a thirteen-year-old in Oregon. I was deeply involved with modern dance in New York at the time and was invited to Rochester for a weekend to meet Minor. Minor's home environment was simple and meaningful: a plain(s) sense of space with tree stumps, rocks, plants, and water was right there in the living room. A few hours after I arrived, Walter Chappell appeared. The whole afternoon and evening subsequently became dominated by my interaction with Walter. Minor remained the onlooker and made no judgments. The weekend culminated with a trip out to the William Gratwick farm.

Walter is one of the fastest photographers I have ever known. He has incredible speed and mastery that conceal technique and equipment. He didn't say much, and most of the time I wasn't aware I was being photographed. There came a point late in the afternoon when I entered the dining room and there were about one hundred fifty photographs of me laid out on a long table. I was a dancer. I had been a model. All the flags of my vanity were flying. Suddenly, I was face to face with all those "selves" of which I was not aware—all the images of all the "Drids": everything from madonna to bitch, from crying child to serene hostess. At that moment (with Walter across the table and Minor and Bill beside me), I knew that I was facing something very important—and somebody who *saw*. It was not Minor at the time but Walter Chappell who wanted to do more photographs. I simply zeroed in on the feeling, and that is where Walt and I were for almost seventy-two hours. I think that I slept for about four hours. It was the kind of moment that is extremely rare.

Minor was an observer to all of this, and I am sure that he restrained Bill from breaking it all up. All the stops were pulled out, as on an organ, and I think that Walter must have made several hundred photographs. I knew later, but did not know then, that some of these involved the movements of Gurdjieff "first obligatories." I could not have had a clearer message that I didn't know who I was or what I was, but the important thing is that this was the kind of thing that could happen in the spaces Minor created. Spiritually, Walt was one of Minor's teachers. I started the Gurdjieff work in 1959 through Walter, who thought I didn't remember anything. But I did remember, not only about the interaction with Walter, but also that without Minor, one of whose greatnesses lay in the ability to create spaces where truly significant things could occur, nothing would have happened.

When you look at me—even now—you are looking at a symbol in Minor's semiotic of that female quality that he spent most of his life trying to come to terms with. There had to be a female element, otherwise the creative process would not have been born, nor would it have matured. Sequence 17, which included his portrait of me in an important sequence because it is the only one, to my way of thinking, that makes sense out of his quest—his inner spaces, which are best understood, perhaps, in terms of the relation between *anima* and *animus*. There was no resolution to Sequence 17. Minor never misled his students into thinking that there was—God knows how many imitation Sequence 17s we'd have had to live with if he had!

I saw Minor five weeks before he died in Boston. I had just returned from Oxford, having seen him the previous autumn in London. He knew he was going to die. The resolution to Sequence 17 was never photographed. It occurred between us, sitting in another living room with the same sense of spaces that his homeplaces always had. He said, "Before I leave, Drid, I have to say that I have misunderstood 'you' all these years. I have done 'you' a disservice, because I always thought your love for me was erotic, which it never was, and I have never seen you until now, but you saw me, didn't you?" When he comprehended *agape* and transcended *eros*, Sequence 17 was completed, by the span of his life.

To get to Minor, you have to try to understand the person who creates spaces. Otherwise, you will be inundated by people who will only tell you what happened to them in those spaces. This man was a creator of spaces with a powerful faith and a guiding hope that he would attract to the life-spaces he created the people, things, and ideas that he wanted to understand and by which he hoped to transform his life. Thus he tried to create spaces where *koans* could happen. I believe that this was crystallized in Rochester when he was deeply involved in trying to understand sequencing and the structures of equivalence. He was applying the apperceptions thus gained to his own life at the same time that he was applying them to photography. And it is all important to note, I think, that meeting Minor was never to feel that his spaces were strange, or *outré*. Minor was real in the common, ordinary sense of that term.

Minor's spaces—outer or inner—were calm. He could talk to many people: consider the range of kinds of person who were in his space and who orbited around him. The space he created did not disregard those who did not understand the *koans* or the intensities of the kinds of inner transformation that I experienced. He honored the social climate of his time, which tended (and still tends) to encourage people to forget or ignore other dimensions. Yet he knew that (some)one has to create spaces in this commonality where deeper, more profound things can happen, because if this isn't done, the commonality can become overpowering. Something is always happening to distract people from the deep quest—the long journey to one's real home: if it isn't the sheer pressure of mundanity, then it is the Crusades, or Vietnam, or the threat of World War III, or the plight of the poor, or something. All of that is mechanical. It simply goes on and on and on. The point is that the Minor Whites of this world, for some unknown reason, consider it a mission, really, to allow those who may be deeply involved in all of this to remember—so they create spaces where that kind of remembering can happen. It becomes a deeply felt moral obligation, especially if one is an artist of Minor's caliber. How else can the statement be made? (And, by the way, it cannot be fabricated, although many try.)

I was attracted to cultural anthropology because, among other things, it deals with the "other" inside and outside one's own society. It is very interesting to be the other in one's own culture: it is both a condition and a psychological state where one possesses at least two maps of the human territory—not one. There is a vertical axis that has to do with levels of be-ing, and there is the horizontal axis of life's progression. The meaning of Minor's life lay on the vertical and not the horizontal axis of his being. Suppose that the conditions of pre-Renaissance art were maintained in our society, specifically the condition of

anonymity, so that artists did not sign their work. How many contemporary artists would still make art, if doing so didn't glorify their individuality and their name? The most profound understanding of Minor White, in my view, consists in the fact that he would have done what he did under any conditions. That, in my opinion, is the test.

Most of the notions about Western art, including photography, are constructed from the point of view of the spectator, which, in the end, is a relatively superficial, or at least incomplete, assessment. Most audiences know nothing about the creation of an artifact. An artist like Minor doesn't think of creating artifacts or art. Spectators of Minor's work (or his life) never comprehended that he worked like a horse day after day. They are usually ignorant of the discipline that the work entailed. Minor's life is a monument to the values of the practice of art, not to the values of the current social institutions of art. Sometimes these are similar, but more often they are not coincidental.

We talked a lot about role playing and conscious role playing as against unconscious role playing in life, and the connections that this may or may not have with the notion of authentic

Walter Chappell, *Minor White, 1957*

Walter Chappell, *Tree Peony Blossoms on Horse Buggy,*
William Gratwick's Estate, Pavilion, N.Y., 1957

human be-ing and about the lives that we haven't lived and the lives that we have lived. But the kind of life that Minor lived that enabled him to produce the extraordinary legacy of his work—the sequences, the equivalents, and all—was not sensational: he didn't use drugs, spend time in a psychiatric hospital, sleep with multitudes of people, or live *la dolce vita,* because if he had he couldn't have practiced his art. He was a plain man, an educated man, and a very shy man, really. He got up, cooked his meals, typed, paid his bills, conversed with people, swept the floor, and spent hundreds of hours in the darkroom. He was what is known in Sufi disciplines as a good householder. You have to be able to manage your house before you can cope successfully with higher levels of spiritual understanding, because those levels don't make anything easier. On the contrary, the traditional routes and paths to enlightenment are always through discipline, and the disciplines of ordinary life are the hardest of all because they are so common. Minor's real life, like that of most great artists, would not make good copy for pulp magazines and sensational journalism, because his real life, like the phoenix, the hoopoe, or the king's falcon, does not come to those who are so deeply immersed in "real life" that they are sleeping when "the other" happens.

WHAT DOES IT MEAN TO BE A CREATOR, to be a *maker* in the true sense? First it means to align oneself: to hold oneself steady in the wind of life, and *see* where others merely notice or running, pass too fast to even notice. Next it means to wake up. To be *awake* means to taste the flavor of things all the way to the pulsebeat and on into the heart of things . . . then further. Again we can go to Minor White who early in his work had been "seized": "Surfaces reveal inner states—cameras record surfaces. Confronted with the world of surfaces in nature, man, and photographs, I must somehow be a kind of microscope by which the underlying forces of Spirit are observed and extended to *others*." (My italics.)

Surfaces (structures, as this might be better named) provide the key to man's innermost being and are the most important link with the world itself as an extension of man. If anyone has ever wondered, Why photographs? White's work will answer his question in an almost awesome way when it is "used" as it has been made to be. In short, photographs (some photographs when made by a master photographer like White who knows exactly what he is doing) X-ray the inner states of things and reveal to us the Why, Is-ness beneath appearances. "For it is in the most eminent degree the province of [real] knowledge, to contemplate the Why" (Aristotle, *Posterior Analytics*, I. 14. 79a23). We leave the merely What behind. We become the true camera; we survey man and the manifestations of Nature and ourselves and we see through our fleshly eye and with the Eye of Spirit, the most subtle Eye that is no *eye*. To *see* with no eye: this is truly the function of all art in relation to man—both as *maker* and *viewer*—and no human being remains locked in the prison of his flesh when he comprehends and participates. . . .

HAVEN O'MORE

Robert Haiko, *Minor White*, 1973

Resemblance reproduces the formal aspects of objects but neglects their spirit; truth shows the spirit and the substance in like perfection. He who tries to transmit the spirit by means of the formal aspect and ends by merely obtaining the outward appearance will produce a dead thing.

CHING HAO

CONTRIBUTORS

ANSEL ADAMS's photographs are currently on view at the Museum of Photographic Art, San Diego, in a major retrospective sponsored by Friends of Photography.

ROBERT ADAMS recently completed *Our Lives and Our Children: Photographs Taken near the Rocky Flats Nuclear Weapons Plant*, published by Aperture. *Summer Nights* will appear in 1985, also from Aperture.

CHARLES ARNOLD is professor of photography at Rochester Institute of Technology.

ROBERT BOURDEAU will have a one-person show of his photographs at the Jane Corkin Gallery in Toronto in the fall, 1984.

ISABEL KANE BRADLEY lives in Ware, Massachusetts and spends her summers on Cape Cod.

HARRY CALLAHAN's "Eleanor and Barbara" is a traveling exhibition sponsored by the Center for Creative Photography.

PAUL CAPONIGRO's latest exhibition, *The Wise Silence*, is a traveling show sponsored by George Eastman House, with an accompanying catalog published by New York Graphic Society.

WALTER CHAPPELL is working on a book of photographs, *Collected Light: The Body of Work*.

CARL CHIARENZA is the Harnish Visiting Artist at Smith College in Massachusetts. His critical biography, *Aaron Siskind: Pleasures and Terrors*, was published in 1982.

JUDY DATER will lead a "Through the Lens" tour in Egypt in the fall.

ABE FRAJNDLICH recently completed a new book of photographs, *Lives I've Never Lived: A Portrait of Minor White*.

ARTHUR FREED is chairman of the Graduate Photography Department at Pratt Institute.

ARNOLD GASSAN is completing his Ph.D. in Guidance and Counseling and is Chairman of Photography, School of Art, Ohio University, Athens.

WILLIAM GILES recently moved to New York City, where he plans to establish a teaching program in photography.

ROBERT HAIKO founded the photography department and is currently teaching photography at Hotchkiss School in Connecticut.

NICHOLAS HLOBECZY is head of the Photography Department at the Cleveland Museum of Art.

DAVID HORTON is assistant professor of photography at Pratt Institute in Brooklyn and recently published with Arthur Freed *In Celebration of the Discovery of the Abandoned Star Factory*.

WILLIAM LARUE teaches elementary school in Oakland, California.

PETER LAYTIN is chairman of the Communications/Media Department at Fitchburg State College, Massachusetts.

ROGER LIPSEY is working on a study of the spiritual dimensions of twentieth-century art, to be published by Shambhala Books.

ROBERT MAHON's multiple piece, *Two Children*, is currently on view in the newly open galleries of The Museum of Modern Art in New York.

BARBARA MORGAN is currently working on a book about energy and movement in photography.

HAVEN O'MORE is director of the Institute of Traditional Science, which supported J.A.B. van Buitenen's new translations of the *Mahābhārata* and the *Bhagavadgitā* published by The University of Chicago Press. O'More, through the Institute, is currently working on a translation of Proclus Diadochus' *Commentaries on Plato's Timaeus*.

SHIRLEY PAUKULIS is a writer-consultant for film and television, a theater performer, and a consultant for visual and performing artists.

EDWARD RANNEY is working with the New Mexico Photographic Survey, an NEA-funded project under the auspices of the Museum of Fine Art in Santa Fe.

EUGENE RICHARDS is working on two new books of photographs, *Exploding into Light* and *The Knife and Gun Club*.

DR. ARNOLD RUSTIN is president of the Oregon Society of Hypnosis in Portland.

AARON SISKIND's photographs are currently on view in a traveling retrospective sponsored by George Eastman House.

FREDERICK SOMMER is writing a collection of essays on the logic of images.

DRID WILLIAMS is associate professor and Director of a graduate program in the anthropology of human movement at New York University. Beginning in August, she will be at Indiana University, Bloomington.

JOHN YANG's one-man shows at the Underground Gallery in the sixties and at the Marcuse Pfeifer Gallery in 1981 are among his major exhibitions.

ACKNOWLEDGMENTS

Many people have generously contributed their time and talents to the creation of this special tribute to Minor White. We are especially grateful to William Parker, R. H. Cravens, Christopher Cox, and Lauren Shakely for editorial contributions in the early stages of the project. Eleanor Caponigro provided special assistance in organizing materials from contributors in the Southwest. Particular thanks are extended to Drid Williams for her time and support. Peter C. Bunnell, Director of the Minor White Archive, the Art Museum, Princeton University, is owed appreciation for his editorial insights and for providing photographs and other materials for the project. To all who submitted photographs and texts we are most grateful.

CREDITS

MINOR WHITE
JUPITER PORTFOLIO

Nude Foot, 1947

Before his death in 1976, Minor White published the *Jupiter Portfolio,*
a collection of twelve silver-gelatin prints of his most important images.
Each print is mounted and overmatted. The edition was planned for one hundred
but only some eighty-nine copies were completed. The prints included are:
Sun Over the Pacific, 1947; *Nude Foot,* 1947; *Sandblaster,* 1949;
Birdlime and Surf, 1951; *Two Barns,* 1955; *Windowsill Daydreaming,* 1958;
Peeled Paint, 1959; *Beginnings,* 1962; *Ritual Stones,* 1963; *Ivy,* 1964;
Navigation Markers, 1970; and *Rock in Snow,* 1971.
A limited number of individual photographs by Minor White are also available.

The portfolio and prints may be viewed by appointment. For additional information contact:
Aperture, Millerton, New York 12546   (518) 789-4491.